INDICATORS OF EDUCATION SYSTEMS

INDICATEURS DES SYSTÈMES
D'ENSEIGNEMENT

PUBLIC EXPECTATIONS OF THE FINAL STAGE OF COMPULSORY EDUCATION

LE DERNIER CYCLE DE L'ENSEIGNEMENT OBLIGATOIRE : QUELLE ATTENTE ?

ORGANISATION FOR ECONOMIC CO-OPERATION AND DEVELOPMENT
ORGANISATION DE COOPÉRATION ET DE DÉVELOPPEMENT ÉCONOMIQUES

ORGANISATION FOR ECONOMIC CO-OPERATION AND DEVELOPMENT

Pursuant to Article 1 of the Convention signed in Paris on 14th December 1960, and which came into force on 30th September 1961, the Organisation for Economic Co-operation and Development (OECD) shall promote policies designed:

- to achieve the highest sustainable economic growth and employment and a rising standard of living in Member countries, while maintaining financial stability, and thus to contribute to the development of the world economy;
- to contribute to sound economic expansion in Member as well as non-member countries in the process of economic development; and
- to contribute to the expansion of world trade on a multilateral, non-discriminatory basis in accordance with international obligations.

The original Member countries of the OECD are Austria, Belgium, Canada, Denmark, France, Germany, Greece, Iceland, Ireland, Italy, Luxembourg, the Netherlands, Norway, Portugal, Spain, Sweden, Switzerland, Turkey, the United Kingdom and the United States. The following countries became Members subsequently through accession at the dates indicated hereafter: Japan (28th April 1964), Finland (28th January 1969), Australia (7th June 1971), New Zealand (29th May 1973) and Mexico (18th May 1994). The Commission of the European Communities takes part in the work of the OECD (Article 13 of the OECD Convention).

The Centre for Educational Research and Innovation was created in June 1968 by the Council of the Organisation for Economic Co-operation and Development and all Member countries of the OECD are participants.

The main objectives of the Centre are as follows:

- *to promote and support the development of research activities in education and undertake such research activities where appropriate;*
- *to promote and support pilot experiments with a view to introducing and testing innovations in the educational system;*
- *to promote the development of co-operation between Member countries in the field of educational research and innovation.*

The Centre functions within the Organisation for Economic Co-operation and Development in accordance with the decisions of the Council of the Organisation, under the authority of the Secretary-General. It is supervised by a Governing Board composed of one national expert in its field of competence from each of the countries participating in its programme of work.

ORGANISATION DE COOPÉRATION ET DE DÉVELOPPEMENT ÉCONOMIQUES

En vertu de l'article 1ᵉʳ de la Convention signée le 14 décembre 1960, à Paris, et entrée en vigueur le 30 septembre 1961, l'Organisation de Coopération et de Développement Économiques (OCDE) a pour objectif de promouvoir des politiques visant :

— à réaliser la plus forte expansion de l'économie et de l'emploi et une progression du niveau de vie dans les pays Membres, tout en maintenant la stabilité financière, et à contribuer ainsi au développement de l'économie mondiale ;

— à contribuer à une saine expansion économique dans les pays Membres, ainsi que les pays non membres, en voie de développement économique ;

— à contribuer à l'expansion du commerce mondial sur une base multilatérale et non discriminatoire conformément aux obligations internationales.

Les pays Membres originaires de l'OCDE sont : l'Allemagne, l'Autriche, la Belgique, le Canada, le Danemark, l'Espagne, les États-Unis, la France, la Grèce, l'Irlande, l'Islande, l'Italie, le Luxembourg, la Norvège, les Pays-Bas, le Portugal, le Royaume-Uni, la Suède, la Suisse et la Turquie. Les pays suivants sont ultérieurement devenus Membres par adhésion aux dates indiquées ci-après : le Japon (28 avril 1964), la Finlande (28 janvier 1969), l'Australie (7 juin 1971), la Nouvelle-Zélande (29 mai 1973) et le Mexique (18 mai 1994). La Commission des Communautés européennes participe aux travaux de l'OCDE (article 13 de la Convention de l'OCDE).

Le Centre pour la Recherche et l'Innovation dans l'Enseignement a été créé par le Conseil de l'Organisation de Coopération et de Développement Économiques en juin 1968 et tous les pays Membres de l'OCDE y participent.

Les principaux objectifs du Centre sont les suivants :

— *encourager et soutenir le développement des activités de recherche se rapportant à l'éducation et entreprendre, le cas échéant, des activités de cette nature ;*

— *encourager et soutenir des expériences pilotes en vue d'introduire des innovations dans l'enseignement et d'en faire l'essai ;*

— *encourager le développement de la coopération entre les pays Membres dans le domaine de la recherche et de l'innovation dans l'enseignement.*

Le Centre exerce son activité au sein de l'Organisation de Coopération et de Développement Économiques conformément aux décisions du Conseil de l'Organisation, sous l'autorité du Secrétaire général et le contrôle direct d'un Comité directeur composé d'experts nationaux dans le domaine de compétence du Centre, chaque pays participant étant représenté par un expert.

Foreword

The General Assembly of the OECD project on International Indicators of Education Systems (INES) met in Lugano, Switzerland, in September 1991. That assembly reviewed the first set of OECD education indicators, and recommended that they be published in *Education at a Glance: OECD Indicators*. After the decision by the CERI Governing Board and the Education Committee in early 1992 to continue to develop education indicators, four networks with voluntary country participation were invited to pursue the conceptual and methodological work needed for the measurement of new indicators in different domains:

- Network A, led by the United States, took up the challenge of developing and measuring indicators of student learning outcomes.
- Network B, with strong support from Sweden, was requested to develop measures of education and labour market destinations.
- Network C, under the leadership of the Netherlands, was given the task of measuring indicators of schools and school processes.
- Network D, supported by the United Kingdom, was invited to chart the expectations and attitudes to education of the various stakeholder groups in OECD societies.

The General Assembly will convene again in June 1995, when Member countries and the people involved in the INES project will take stock of what has been achieved, examine the organisational framework of the sets of indicators produced so far, and explore the possibilities for further developments. To facilitate this review, each network has prepared a report describing the conceptual, methodological, and policy problems encountered in constructing its respective clusters of indicators. The four reports are presented to the INES General Assembly as background and reference documents. Collectively, they offer a rich account of innovations, successes and failures in indicator development at the OECD, information that is essential for a review of perspectives and options for possible future work.

The content of each report has been discussed and endorsed during plenary sessions of the networks. The contributors are mostly members and national delegates to the networks, although in some cases distinguished independent experts have also contributed. For each network, members reviewed all the papers and suggested modifications where needed.

The international study reported in this volume was made possible thanks to the support received from the United Kingdom, the lead country of Network D, and particularly the Scottish Office, which generously contributed to the study and co-ordinated the production of this report. The financial contributions made by EUROSTAT and the US National Center for Education Statistics are also gratefully acknowledged.

This volume was prepared by the network Chair, Her Majesty's Chief Inspector Archie McGlynn of the Scottish Office Education Department, Edinburgh, with the assistance of John MacBeath of the University of Strathclyde, Glasgow, in co-operation with Norberto Bottani and Albert Tuijnman of the OECD Secretariat.

This report is published on the responsibility of the Secretary-General of the OECD. It represents the views of the authors and does not necessarily reflect those of the OECD or of its Member countries.

Avant-propos

L'Assemblée générale du projet de l'OCDE sur les indicateurs internationaux des systèmes d'enseignement (INES) s'est réunie à Lugano, en Suisse, en septembre 1991. Elle a passé en revue la première série d'indicateurs de l'enseignement de l'OCDE et recommandé qu'ils soient publiés dans *Regards sur l'éducation : les indicateurs de l'OCDE*. Après que le Comité directeur du CERI et le Comité de l'éducation eurent décidé au début de 1992 de poursuivre l'élaboration d'indicateurs de l'enseignement, quatre réseaux, auxquels les pays participent volontairement, ont été invités à effectuer les travaux conceptuels et méthodologiques nécessaires pour mesurer de nouveaux indicateurs dans différents domaines :

- Le Réseau A, mené par les Etats-Unis, s'est donné pour mission d'élaborer et de mesurer des indicateurs des acquis des élèves et étudiants.
- Le Réseau B, qui bénéficie d'une importante aide de la Suède, a été invité à mettre au point des mesures relatives à l'enseignement et aux débouchés professionnels.
- Le Réseau C, dirigé par les Pays-Bas, s'est vu confier la tâche de mesurer les indicateurs des établissements et des processus scolaires.
- Le Réseau D, soutenu par le Royaume-Uni, a été invité à décrire les attentes et les attitudes à l'égard de l'enseignement des diverses parties prenantes dans les pays de l'OCDE.

L'Assemblée générale se réunira de nouveau en juin 1995, ce qui permettra aux pays Membres et aux personnes participant au projet INES de faire le bilan de ce qui a été accompli, d'examiner l'organisation des séries d'indicateurs élaborés jusqu'à présent, et d'étudier les prolongements possibles. Pour faciliter cet examen, chaque réseau décrit dans un rapport les problèmes conceptuels, méthodologiques et politiques auxquels il s'est heurté dans la construction de sa propre série d'indicateurs. Les quatre rapports sont présentés à l'Assemblée générale du projet INES à titre de documents de référence. Ensemble, ils rendent compte en détail des innovations introduites avec ou sans succès dans la construction d'indicateurs à l'OCDE, autant d'informations qui sont essentielles pour étudier les perspectives et les options qui s'offrent en vue de la poursuite des travaux.

Le contenu de chaque rapport a été examiné et approuvé au cours des sessions plénières des réseaux. Les auteurs sont dans leur majorité des membres des réseaux et des personnes déléguées près d'eux par les pays, encore que dans certains cas des experts indépendants de haut niveau aient aussi apporté leur concours. Pour chacun des réseaux, les membres ont passé en revue tous les rapports et, le cas échéant, suggéré des modifications.

Ce rapport a été élaboré grâce à l'aide reçue du Royaume-Uni qui a assuré la direction du Réseau D, et en particulier le Scottish Office, qui a généreusement contribué à sa publication et en a assuré la coordination. Nous remercions vivement EUROSTAT et le National Center for Education Statistics des États-Unis pour leur contribution financière.

Ce volume a été établi par le président du réseau, Archie McGlynn, Inspecteur en chef des écoles, du Département de l'Éducation du Scottish Office, Edimbourg, avec l'aide de John MacBeath de l'Université de Strathclyde, Glasgow, en coopération avec Norberto Bottani et Albert Tuijnman du Secrétariat de l'OCDE.

Ce rapport est publié sous la responsabilité du Secrétaire général de l'OCDE. Il reflète les opinions des auteurs et ne représente pas nécessairement le point de vue de l'OCDE ni celui de ses pays Membres.

Table of Contents/Table des matières

Chapter/Chapitre 3

A Conceptual Framework: The Rationale for Attitude Indicators
Un cadre théorique : la justification des indicateurs d'attitude

Alain Michel and John MacBeath

Chapter/Chapitre 4

The Policy Context: A Summary
Résumé du contexte de politique générale

Laura Salganik and Lillian King

Chapter/Chapitre 5

Design of the Study
Conception de l'étude

Roel Bosker and Roger Thomas

Chapter/Chapitre 6
The Findings
Principaux résultats de l'enquête
Carol Calvert and John MacBeath

Chapter/Chapitre 7
Interpreting the Findings
Interprétation des résultats
John MacBeath and Carol Calvert

Introduction

by

Archie McGlynn
Her Majesty's Chief Inspector of Schools,
Scottish Office Education Department,
Edinburgh, Scotland

John MacBeath and Carol Calvert argue in Chapter 7 that the seven indicators to be published in 1995 in *Education at a Glance* "are only the tip of an iceberg whose bulk lies below the water line" (see Annex 1 to this volume). This substantial piece of work, together with Network D's technical report (see Bosker, 1995), is testimony to the truth of their assessment. Moreover, any evaluation of the network's contribution to the continuing success of INES has to recognise that it has led to the creation of twelve national reports, analytic and evaluative in style, which have provoked responses in policy discussions in the twelve participating countries.

Those commentators, and there were several in the early days when the network was struggling to define its mission and launch the work necessary for its accomplishment, who told us that our desire for international indicators of attitudes was virtually an impossible idea to translate into practice, merely succeeded in uniting the network. There was a singleness of purpose about the network: to work together to produce a set of attitude indicators which would stand up to public scrutiny, complement the existing INES set, and add a new dimension to international comparisons.

In the end, the coming together of the seven indicators, this report and the technical report was a team effort. It was a privilege to be *primus inter pares* in a network which thrived on debate and encouraged openness. The informality fostered a frank discussion and easier challenge when there was honest disagreement in our deliberations. If asked to describe the ethos of Network D meetings, I think members would characterise it as strenuous and clearly focused, friendly and enjoyable. My thanks to all of Network D, past and present. We could not have succeeded without the commitment of Member countries.

It takes considerable support, both financial and otherwise, to run an international network. In the United Kingdom context, Virginia Berkeley and her colleagues in the

Department for Education, were always on hand. A special thanks to my colleagues in the HM Inspectors of Schools Audit Unit, to my project manager Carol Calvert, and to my associate editor Professor John MacBeath. Above all I am grateful to my employers, the Scottish Office Education Department, for financing, supporting and encouraging our work at all times.

Introduction

par

Archie McGlynn
Inspecteur en chef des écoles,
Département de l'Éducation du Scottish Office,
Edimbourg, Écosse

John MacBeath et Carol Calvert affirment au chapitre 7 que les sept indicateurs publiés dans la version de 1995 de *Regards sur l'éducation* ne constituent que la pointe d'un iceberg dont la plus grande partie est invisible (voir annexe 1 du présent ouvrage). Cet ouvrage considérable, de même que le rapport technique du Réseau D (voir Bosker, 1995), témoignent de la justesse de leur évaluation. De plus, toute évaluation de la contribution du réseau au succès continu du projet INES sur les indicateurs internationaux des systèmes d'enseignement doit prendre en compte les douze rapports nationaux de type analytique et estimatif qui en ont résulté et qui ont suscité des réactions dans le cadre du débat de politique générale mené dans les douze pays participants.

Plusieurs de ces commentateurs – et notamment dans les premiers temps, lorsque le réseau s'efforçait de définir sa mission et d'entreprendre le travail nécessaire à sa réalisation – qui nous ont dit que notre désir de disposer d'indicateurs internationaux de comportement était pratiquement impossible à réaliser, ont en fait réussi à unir le réseau. Celui-ci avait un objectif bien défini : collaborer pour établir un ensemble d'indicateurs de comportement qui puisse résister à un examen public, compléter la série d'indicateurs internationaux des systèmes d'enseignement existante et ajouter une nouvelle dimension aux comparaisons internationales.

La mise au point des sept indicateurs, du présent rapport et du rapport technique est le fruit d'un effort collectif. Ce fut un privilège que de participer en tant que « premier entre ses pairs » aux travaux d'un réseau qui encourageait la discussion et l'ouverture d'esprit. Son caractère informel et amical a favorisé une discussion franche et facilité les débats. Que tous les membres du Réseau D ainsi que les pays Membres en soient remerciés.

Nous tenons également à remercier Virginia Berkeley et ses collègues du Département de l'Éducation du Royaume-Uni pour leur grande disponibilité, ainsi que nos collègues du Service de l'inspection scolaire, Carol Calvert, qui a dirigé le projet, et John MacBeath qui en a été le rédacteur associé. Un remerciement tout particulier doit être ici adressé au Département de l'Éducation du Scottish Office pour avoir constamment financé, soutenu et encouragé nos travaux.

The Birth of a Network
Naissance d'un réseau

by

John MacBeath
University of Strathclyde, Scotland

and

Archie McGlynn
Scottish Office Education Department, Edinburgh, Scotland

This opening chapter charts the phases of development in the life of Network D, illustrating the process by which a network, at first, slowly struggles to make sense of things and to find its own identity, and then moves with increasing confidence towards its goals. It identifies critical points in decision-making, considers procedures and structures which enable work to progress, and describes how, in different phases of a network's life, its morale and self-identity is sustained and nurtured. It concludes with some lessons learned about international co-operation of this nature.

*

*   *

Note de synthèse

Ce chapitre d'introduction décrit les différentes phases de la vie d'un réseau, depuis le combat initial pour donner un sens à son rôle et lui donner une identité jusqu'au stade auquel on peut définir avec davantage de confiance ses objectifs et les réaliser.

Le Réseau D a commencé par un ensemble d'ouvrages théoriques sur les attitudes vis-à-vis d'une scolarisation efficace, ce que l'on en attend, ainsi que les conclusions des recherches à ce sujet. Bien qu'un débat instructif ait pu ainsi avoir lieu, le réseau a adopté en 1990 une approche plus pragmatique en rassemblant des données sur ce que l'on faisait effectivement dans différents pays pour évaluer les attitudes et les attentes des différents groupes. Ce travail s'est avéré utile et a abouti à un «plan comparatif» qui a permis aux membres du réseau d'avoir une vue d'ensemble des groupes cibles, des méthodologies et des centres d'intérêt dans différents pays.

Cette vue d'ensemble a constitué un point de départ utile pour identifier les préoccupations communes et cerner une série de problèmes fondamentaux sur lesquels tous les pays Membres souhaitaient rassembler des données. Au sujet de ces préoccupations communes, on s'est mis d'accord sur les personnes à consulter, par exemple la population en général, les parents, les enseignants et les élèves. Pour pouvoir incorporer les indicateurs du Réseau D dans Regards sur l'éducation (1995), il a été décidé que l'on ne pourrait faire une enquête que sur un seul des groupes cibles et qu'il était absolument prioritaire de connaître les vues de la population en général. A certains égards, c'était là le point de départ le plus facile compte tenu de l'existence d'organismes d'étude de marché et de moyens d'enquête dans la plupart des pays participants.

Le réseau s'est alors concentré sur l'établissement d'un questionnaire. Il a déployé, au cours des mois suivants, des efforts considérables pour se mettre d'accord sur une présentation, des catégories de réponses, des éléments de questionnaire communs et pour faire en sorte que le vocabulaire et le style employés correspondent dans tous les pays. Le fait que la Finlande, la Belgique et les Pays-Bas aient proposé de jouer un rôle pilote pour établir le questionnaire a aidé à préciser une méthodologie et également à définir les tâches exactes à entreprendre. La décision de nommer des sous-groupes techniques chargés de faire avancer les travaux a été importante car elle a permis d'accomplir un travail intensif et bien défini. Tout aussi importante a été la décision de nommer un directeur de projet au sein du Scottish Office d'Edimbourg et d'utiliser une méthode critique qui a permis de fixer la date de communication finale des indicateurs. L'Université de Twente aux Pays-Bas a été chargée d'établir la base de données internationales en collaboration étroite avec la nouvelle Analysis Unit d'Edimbourg et le Social and Community Planning Research (SCPR) de Londres.

L'année 1994 a correspondu à la phase la plus intensive du projet, durant laquelle on s'est employé essentiellement à recueillir des données auprès de tous les pays, à les analyser, à les traduire en indicateurs et à chercher des moyens de présenter ceux-ci sous une forme expressive et accessible. En six mois, les indicateurs ont été révisés à plusieurs reprises jusqu'à ce que le réseau dispose de sept présentations sous forme de textes et d'images dont tous les membres ont pu constater avec satisfaction qu'ils étaient parfaitement conformes à leurs intentions. Outre la satisfaction due au fait de disposer d'un produit fini de bonne qualité, le processus d'élaboration proprement dit a donné aux membres du réseau la possibilité d'apprendre en illustrant les différentes phases par lesquelles passe un groupe international.

Pour terminer, ce chapitre examine l'importance des principes déontologiques à établir pour permettre un échange franc et fructueux d'idées et assurer l'équilibre voulu entre le travail et le jeu, le formalisme et un style informel. Il en conclut que cela a aidé à instaurer un véritable climat de respect professionnel et d'estime mutuelle entre les membres du réseau.

*

* *

1. The Beginnings of the Network

Network D, the newest network of the INES project, was invited to develop indicators which would say something about the views of the people most closely involved in using schools, in paying for schools and in making them work. In more technical language, Network D has been concerned with indicators of attitudes and expectations of the key players in the school system. The purpose of developing such indicators would be to illuminate and complement the outcome, process and context indicators produced by Networks A, B and C. By the end of 1994 Network D was, in fact, able to offer an initial set of indicators for inclusion in *Education at a Glance* (OECD, 1995; see Annex 1 to this volume). Membership rose during the life of the network from seven to fourteen. The Netherlands was the lead country in the earlier years, giving way to the current lead nation, the United Kingdom, at the General Assembly of 1991, held in Lugano.

2. First Steps in the Growth of the Network

The original seven Member countries were Belgium (Flemish Community), France, Italy, the Netherlands, Switzerland, the United Kingdom and the United States. The first year and more of Network D was taken up with theoretical debate and with the attempt to define indicators on the basis of research literature. As their starting point, the Member countries looked to the considerable body of work in the area of attitudes and expectations and the substantial body of literature on effective schooling. While providing an instructive and often rich debate within the network, it did not lead members much closer to the goal of defining a usable set of indicators. So, in the early 1990s the network decided to adopt a more pragmatic approach. It took as its starting point what was actually being done in the various Member countries to gauge the attitudes and expectations of students, parents, teachers, the general public and employers.

The network identified a given time period (1985-90) and asked each Member country to examine all the surveys of attitudes and expectations that had been conducted nationally during that period. The target groups for these surveys were to be school students, teachers, parents, the general public, and employers. This approach was less concerned with the theoretical justification for indicators than the policy implications of national surveys and studies. If there were surveys being conducted, what was the impetus for these? How did they feed into the policy-making process and into public and professional consciousness? Specifically, this exercise would answer the following questions:

- What kinds of attitudes are Member countries interested in surveying?
- What is the survey vehicle used?
- What is the purpose of seeking this information?
- Who is it that seeks to collect that information?
- To whom do they put their questions?
- What kind of questions do they actually ask?
- What is the size of sample?

A small working group from Belgium (Flemish Community), the Netherlands and the United Kingdom collated and analysed the data, putting it together into a document which came to be known as "the comparative plan" and which marked a first significant step forward by the network.

Table 1.1 shows some examples of comparable national attitudes surveys.

The extent of the survey data that already existed in each of the Member countries came to most people as a considerable surprise. The exercise had proved its worth in demonstrating the interest and impetus that already existed, but it served another function too. It was able to identify vehicles which might be used by Member countries for "piggy-backing" on (i.e. riding on the back of) existing, proven surveys. For example, the annual survey of *British Social Attitudes* on a range of social issues offered a ready-made vehicle for the United Kingdom. It was these "iterative" surveys that were of

Table/Tableau 1.1.

Some national attitudes surveys

Sélection d'enquêtes nationales sur les comportements

Title	Country	Scope
Conditions of life and aspirations of the French	France	2 000 general public
Reasons for choice of school and opinions about education	Netherlands	2 000 parents
Attitudes and expectations of in-service training of teachers in middle schools in Lombardy	Italy	2 004 parents
Public attitudes towards the public schools	US	1 598 general public
Parental awareness of school education	UK	2 000 parents
Motivation and demotivation in secondary education: student characteristics	Belgium (Flemish Community)	2 699 students
Experience with heterogeneous classes	Switzerland	1 678 students 1 594 parents

Source: OECD, INES project.

20

particular interest to the network because they offered future and long-term possibilities for incorporating the network's own survey questions on a continuing basis.

3. The Development of an Identity and Purpose

The next step forward was taken at a meeting in the Hague in 1991 when the network started to sift through the data gathered in order to identify common themes which might serve as the basis for indicators. This identification of "common concerns" marked a watershed in the life of Network D because it brought with it the realisation that all countries shared a common core of private values and public concerns (a fuller treatment of "common concerns" is provided in the following chapter). It brought both a social bonding of the membership and, for the first time, offered to members a clear and shared vision of where the network might be going, although it remained unclear how to get there.

By the time of the General Assembly of INES in Lugano in late 1991, the network had compiled a short, succinct report entitled *Common Concerns* (MacBeath, 1991) and a 70-page document entitled *Towards Attitudinal Indicators* (MacBeath *et al.*, 1991). As well as providing important working documents for the network itself, these also offered to other networks an insight into the goals, procedures and achievements of the network to date. Using the framework of the seven common concerns, they illustrated the kinds of survey that had been conducted in different countries, drawing examples from different target groups and different sample sizes.

The Lugano meeting gave the network a mandate for the future: it was now time to translate "concerns" into specific indicators and into strategies and techniques.

Figure 1.1 summarises the inter-relationship of the various phases of work and the path to indicators.

4. The Expansion of the Network

The Lugano meeting generated interest among other countries, and the network was given encouragement and further impetus by the addition of Denmark, Finland, Spain and Sweden. Soon after, the network grew even further with the addition of the French Community of Belgium, Portugal and Turkey. They joined the seven existing countries for the first meeting in Paris in 1992 under the direction of the United Kingdom as lead country, although of these three, only Portugal took part in the network survey. At that Paris meeting, new members were alerted to the importance of early contact with policy-makers, and all countries were charged with sounding out policy-makers and budget holders at the earliest opportunity so that tangible progress could be made towards the network's goals in the coming year. The Paris meeting established clear goals – to provide a first set of indicators for inclusion in *Education at a Glance* (OECD, 1995) and to focus on the needs of policy-makers.

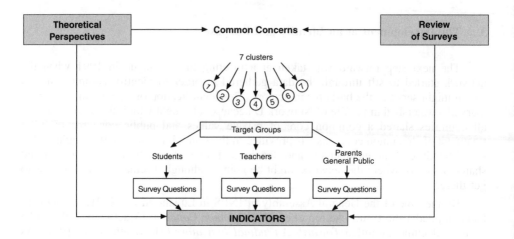

Figure/*Graphique* 1.1. **Common concerns**
Préoccupations communes

Source: OECD, INES project.

5. The Determination of the Network's Focus

A significant milestone for the network was its 1992 meeting in Edinburgh, at which a decision had to be made about an action agenda based on the goals agreed in Paris. What would be the contribution on attitudes and expectations? It was realised by members that although the timeline from 1992 to 1994 looked generous, there was in fact the need for a very fast and effective response if that deadline was to be met.

The network split into small sub-groups, each to come back with an argument for focusing on teachers, students, parents or the general public as a first target group. The presentations by these groups back to the whole group were absorbing and imaginative, but at the end it was "the general public" that won. This decision was to some extent taken on pragmatic grounds:

- Surveys of the general public could, within a relatively short time-scale, be conducted in all Member countries.
- There were already, in most countries, existing vehicles for such surveys ("piggy-backing").
- Surveys showed that policy-makers were interested in the views of the general public.
- It would be least disruptive of schools.

- It would give the network experience and provide an important first step on which to build for the future.

Once the decision was made to concentrate on the views of the general public, a number of other questions followed:
- What kind of views would be sought?
- How would they be gathered?
- How would comparability be dealt with?
- What would be the time-scale?
- How much would it cost?

The reference point was the *Common Concerns* identified in the Hague and written up in English and French as a working document. The network decided to look primarily at five of the areas of common concern:
- expectations of, and satisfaction with, schools' priority goals;
- expectations of, and satisfaction with, the curriculum;
- attitudes to locus of decision-making in schools;
- expectations of the role of the school and the home in personal/social education; and
- perceptions of teacher status and morale.

Out of this a working draft of a questionnaire was developed which was to become the basis for the network's proposed survey.

This having been agreed, the next phase of the work was, back in Member countries, to proceed as fast as possible to investigate the resources of each country to carry out such a survey, and to ensure the political will to do so within a relatively tight time-scale. For the lead country, the challenge was to make specific proposals on the style, nature and size of the questionnaire, and to establish a communication system and a consultancy on technical and language issues, both of these acknowledged by members to be complex and demanding. Communication is the rock on which international networks can easily perish. A commitment to efficient relaying of information and fast response was agreed by members. It was, from the Edinburgh meeting onwards, a significant feature of the network's operation.

6.   The Finalisation of the Survey Questionnaire

The next network meeting, in El Escorial, Spain, had the task of finally agreeing the structure and format of the questionnaire. Since the previous meeting in Edinburgh, there had been heavy traffic between the lead country and Member countries, negotiating and reformulating questions in an attempt to ensure that the meeting in Spain would move the network nearer its goals. The sharing and dialogue opened up a number of new issues.

Essentially, these issues had to do with cultural conventions, language, and the framing of questions: questions about school priorities in, for example, examination success, and preparation for work and for the world (citizenship). Should the questionnaire include items about religious education? Was the question on teachers' salaries too political to be asked in some countries? There were also issues to do with the timing of questionnaires, which had to take account of local politics and elections. There were difficulties with one or two countries in getting agreement from policy-makers, a need to proceed fast in some countries and a recognition that in others the process was going to be a slow one. An offer from Finland to pilot the questionnaire was gratefully accepted, as was the offer by the Belgians and Dutch to translate and pilot a joint Dutch-language version for use in both countries. The initiatives helped considerably in testing the validity and robustness of the questionnaire items, the language used, and the receptivity of the public to this form of survey.

The specificity of the target group and the tangible product of a finalised questionnaire (see Annex 2 to this volume) brought home some of the financial and political realities. They also gave a sharpness of focus to the meeting, and members left El Escorial with a clear agenda and in some cases, a considerable amount of work to do back in their own countries.

7. The Value of Sub-groups

At the end of the El Escorial meeting, technical and presentation sub-groups were elected to take forward key tasks and to prepare the ground for the next full meeting in Paris in November, 1993. The sub-groups met in Edinburgh in September 1993, and it became quickly apparent to the participants that the network was faced with a major challenge – how to handle the very large amount of data that would be generated, to process and analyse it and carry it forward to the formulation of indicators and, ultimately, their presentation in *Education at a Glance*. In other words, to carry out an ambitious task in a complex aspect of education and in a time-scale unheard of in international studies or projects. Cost implications also figured large in the discussions.

It was recognised that a key to achieving the task which the network had set itself would be the appointment of a project manager to assist the network Chair, based in a new Analysis Unit in Edinburgh, and the setting up of a database in the University of Twente. This was agreed, and the lead country set about strengthening its team with co-operation from other countries.

The sub-group (further sub-dividing into smaller working groups) produced:
* a job description for the project manager;
* a remit for the Analysis Unit (to be headed by the project manager);
* an outline for the database and other technical requirements such as a questionnaire analysis code book;
* a one-year critical path analysis up to the final delivery of indicators;
* a costing analysis; and
* a draft outline of the report for the annual assembly.

These decisions were presented to, and ratified by, the whole network in the meeting in Paris attended by the newly-appointed project manager from the Scottish Office. The extensive experience of the United States in this work was also recognised and made available to the United Kingdom. It marked the beginning of a close working relationship between the lead country, the University of Twente and the United States in data collection and analysis. Countries co-operated on translation: for example, Spain with Portugal, and the Netherlands with Belgium (Flemish Community); the Nordic countries pooled ideas and experience; and France's wide experience of public opinion surveys was made available to the lead country.

8.   The Implementation and Analysis of the Survey

The database "shell" was constructed at the University of Twente in conjunction with the Analysis Unit in Edinburgh, drawing on results from the first three completed surveys. This was then passed to the project manager in Scotland, who processed country returns as they arrived. Between May 1993 and April 1994, all twelve countries carried out their national surveys *i.e.* the fourteen members of Network D with the exceptions of Belgium (French Community), Italy and Turkey. As new data were added and processed, patterns began to emerge, so that, simultaneously with the analysis of data, indicators and ways of presenting them began to suggest themselves. All of this involved close co-operation between the lead country, the University of Twente and the network's technical advisers, Social and Community Planning Research, London.

As a result of coming and going between countries, exchange of ideas, expert advice from, for example, the Netherlands, Spain and the United States, and painstaking work in the Analysis Unit, the lead country presented a long list of indicators – eight "probables", six "possibles" and 17 "others" – to the Technical/Presentation sub-group, which met in New Orleans in April 1994. In two intensive days in New Orleans, many new possibilities were opened up, examined, sometimes discarded and sometimes added to the existing core group of preferred indicators. The ten "probables" remaining at the end of the two days had been through an exhaustive examination.

Between that April meeting in New Orleans and the full network meeting in Washington in June, refining of the indicators continued. As data from the twelve participating countries arrived, they threw new light on the indicator set. A new list of "probable" indicators was composed for the Washington meeting, where the indicators were again subjected to close scrutiny together with the accompanying descriptors for *Education at a Glance* (OECD, 1995). How to present indicators, whether to show countries alphabetically or in ascending or descending order of importance were, on the surface, issues of presentation but beneath lay significant educational and political issues.

The target, to deliver a set of indicators for inclusion in *Education at a Glance* was more or less achieved in Washington. However, it would be misleading to see all the investment and energy of its members as measured by that outcome alone. There have been tangible benefits to countries involved. These include:

- sharing and developing expertise in the conduct and interpretation of surveys;
- establishment of links and networks for the exchange of information and expertise;

- creation of channels for dissemination of the wider INES project;
- provision of consultancy to Member countries for use in internal policy-making and school improvement initiatives; and
- professional development and widening of the perspectives of individuals involved.

9.   Nursing the Network

The duty falls to the lead country, and to the chair specifically, to try simultaneously to meet five objectives:

- to keep the network focused on its task and members aware of its progress towards its goals;
- to maintain the morale of the group as a whole and to help to blend members into a coherent team – to create a network ethos;
- to look to the differing needs of individual members and ensure their participation and contribution;
- to build-in quality control at all stages; and
- to promote and develop good links with the INES Secretariat and the leaders of country teams in the network.

Network D has tried to achieve this balance and has found it useful to move between full group and small group sessions. Sub-groups were mandated by the whole network to undertake certain tasks over a period of time, in some cases between one and two years. Sub-groups in Network D have tackled three main tasks: standardisation of question-naires, language and methodology; analysis; and selection of indicators.

It was realised within the network that expert sub-groups carry with them a risk in terms of their ownership and the morale of the rest of the members. For example, sub-group members can move ahead in knowledge and experience of the issues, and then either dominate full meetings or inhibit other members' contributions. The responsibilities and contributions of all individual participants therefore had to be maintained and sub-group members were made aware of the need to "make space" for others.

Common Concerns
Préoccupations communes

by

John MacBeath
University of Strathclyde, Scotland

This chapter describes the common concerns identified by the network at a seminal meeting in the Hague in 1991. The exploration and discovery of common concerns was important both for the morale of network members and because it gave a clear focus and direction for everyone involved. It provided the foundation stone on which all subsequent work was built, and from which the first indicators of attitudes emerged in 1994. Each of the relevant areas is dealt with in turn, summarising the range of relevant issues and source of the key questions that would be included within a questionnaire.

*

*   *

Note de synthèse

Le deuxième chapitre reprend le thème des « préoccupations communes » (MacBeath, 1991) et décrit comment celles-ci ont été identifiées et examinées par le réseau.

Au cours des premières réunions du réseau, les participants ont consacré beaucoup de temps et d'énergie à la recherche d'un langage commun pour concilier des différences au niveau des systèmes, des structures et des conceptions de la vie scolaire, et également en ce qui concerne les programmes et les relations entre l'univers scolaire et le monde du travail.

Ces différences n'excluaient pas, cependant, des préoccupations et une conception communes de l'apprentissage ainsi que du financement et de la gestion des écoles. L'identification de ces préoccupations communes a été une étape importante pour le réseau car elle a permis d'établir un ordre du jour et de mettre en lumière les travaux à poursuivre. Cette tâche a été considérablement simplifiée par les efforts déployés dans chaque pays pour identifier les enquêtes qui avaient été effectuées au cours des cinq années précédentes (1985-90), et par l'analyse des thèmes abordés dans le cadre de ces enquêtes.

Les membres du réseau ont été divisés en sous-groupes chargés d'identifier les questions à examiner en commun. Plusieurs ensembles de préoccupations communes ont été identifiées :

• la profession d'enseignant ;
• la gestion des écoles ;
• les programmes scolaires ;
• les rapports entre élèves et enseignants ;
• la communication ;
• l'égalité ;
• la politique de l'éducation.

Il ne s'agissait pas de sept domaines distincts mais plutôt de rubriques utiles permettant de délimiter des questions clés. Certains des problèmes traités dans le cadre de chacune de ces sept rubriques consistaient à définir le contenu de l'enquête auprès de la population en général, en s'inspirant des travaux effectués dans certains des pays participants qui avaient sondé le public et d'autres groupes-cibles sur ces questions. Les problèmes identifiés dans le cadre de ces sept rubriques étaient notamment les suivants.

La rubrique « la profession d'enseignant » regroupait certains problèmes liés au statut et au moral des enseignants. Sous la rubrique « gestion des écoles », certains problèmes concernaient la direction et les objectifs de l'école. La rubrique « programmes scolaires » recouvrait toute une série de problèmes et notamment les programmes prévus, ceux qui sont effectivement suivis et les rapports entre ceux-ci et la vie et le travail. La rubrique « rapports entre élèves et enseignants » incluait ce que les enseignants attendaient des élèves et vice-versa. La catégorie « communications » comprenait la communication des politiques et des priorités scolaires et l'efficacité des informations fournies aux parents par les écoles. Sous la rubrique « égalité » figuraient les problèmes liés à la satisfaction de besoins particuliers, à un traitement équitable et à l'égalité des chances. La rubrique « politique d'éducation » couvrait les dépenses et le processus de décision concernant l'éducation et l'efficacité avec laquelle le système atteint ses principaux objectifs.

Dans ces sept domaines d'intérêt commun, les travaux prévus représentaient pour le réseau un programme d'action ambitieux. Ces travaux ont commencé par une série de questions à poser au public dans chaque pays Membre.

*

*   *

1. Getting Beneath the Differences

In the search for common indicators of performance across a range of countries, the single greatest challenge is the variety of policy and practice from one country to the next. School structures differ considerably, in the way in which teachers are trained. Their job definition is not always similar, nor are the responsibilities they are expected to carry. There are differences in what children learn, when and where they learn it, and how that learning is assessed. There are differences in the role of parents in the education of their children, and in the way schools communicate with them. The point at which the world of the school meets the world of work varies from country to country, and the way in which the curriculum reflects the larger social and economic context differs too.

Yet, these differences are in many respects only on the surface. Beneath there lie common concerns which seem to be integral to the provision of public education. This is because education is essentially about people and about how people relate to one another. There is also a common body of wisdom about learning and teaching, and a common set of issues about the financing and managing of educational institutions within advanced economies.

The recognition of these underlying similarities and the identification of common concerns was the task undertaken in the Hague in February 1991. Member countries brought to that meeting their own inventories of polls and surveys conducted between 1985 and 1990, which were to be used as the basis for abstracting common concerns. Working through sub-groups, it was found that the many issues could be grouped into seven broad clusters. These clusters did not represent seven discrete areas, but broad, overlapping areas of concern. The clustering itself is, however, of secondary importance, serving as a temporary device, leading the network towards key questions and key indicators on which all countries could agree.

The broad clusters were:

- teaching as a profession;
- the management of schools;
- the curriculum;
- student-teacher relationships;
- communications;
- equality and equity; and
- education policy.

Each of these seven contained within it a number of different but related issues.

2. The Common Concerns

Teaching as a Profession

This first cluster of issues includes:

- the quality of teachers;

- teacher status and morale;
- the professionalisation of teaching;
- teacher training;
- the appraisal or evaluation of teacher performance; and
- teachers' ability and willingness to cope with innovation and change.

Common to all countries is a perception of teaching as a profession. These perceptions may not always be close to reality, but are in many ways more important and powerful than the reality. It was found that a number of countries were already conducting surveys comparing teachers to other professional groups, for example.

Survey questions included: What is the attitude to teaching as a career? What kind of professional training is regarded as appropriate in comparison with other professions? What form of accountability do parents (or the public) expect from teachers? What are seen as the most significant qualities of a good teacher?

The Management of Schools

A number of issues centre on how schools are run. They focus on questions of effectiveness, and this includes questions about: school leadership; sharing of the goals of the school; school climate/ethos/culture; and partnerships (for example, with parents or with students).

School leadership takes different forms from country to country, and the significance of the leader (the head or principal) varies too. What is fruitful to this enquiry is to ask about the importance of leadership in setting the purposes, priorities, and ethos of the school, and to identify perceptions of where that leadership is seen to be located. The degree to which students and parents are seen as playing a role in school management may also be an important variable. These are potentially useful international comparisons in respect of the perceived role of parents and students, as well as perceptions of their influence in educational decision-making.

A significant issue in all countries is how pathways in education and transitions from one level to the next are managed by the students, particularly at key stages, such as from first to second-level education, or at key points of choosing a course or career. Again, it is how influential players perceive these transitions which may be the most useful kind of evidence. Some questions relating to the governance and management of schools, which point to areas for which indicators might usefully be developed, are:

- What are seen as the most important purposes of schools?
- What are seen as the most important priorities of schools?
- Are schools judged to be meeting those purposes and priorities?
- Are schools seen as fostering a positive attitude to learning?
- What are regarded as the most important aspects of a good school ethos?
- How significant is the role of the headteacher/principal in relation to the schools' goals, and in establishing a school climate?
- What are the public (parents', teachers', students') attitudes to the involvement of parents in schools?

The Curriculum

Under the broad heading of "the curriculum" there are a range of issues covering what pupils learn, what teachers teach, and how these relate to life beyond the school gates. The issues include:

- the quality of the curriculum;
- the intended curriculum;
- the achieved curriculum, the achievement of students; and
- the relationship of the curriculum to life and to work.

The curriculum relates to what is planned for learners, and it describes the relationship between that and what is to be taught by teachers. This "grand plan" is referred to as the "intended curriculum" and is, in many countries, conceived at a national or state level. What that curriculum ought to be, and how well it represents what people think ought to be learned in schools, is a common issue for all countries.

Perhaps even more of a common concern is the confidence that people have in schools' delivery of the curriculum. This is sometimes described as "the achieved curriculum" and refers to the nature and quality of what students actually learn. Parents or employers might have concerns about the advantage of the achieved curriculum to working life, or to personal or social development. Differences in achievement from school to school, or from group to group, are of concern in all countries, and the phenomenon of the "drop-out", and who drops out, is an international issue. Some of the specific questions under this heading are:

- What do students wish to learn?
- What do parents want for their children?
- What do employers regard as important?
- Are school achievements valued by students, parents, employers and the general public?
- Is the curriculum seen as providing skills and knowledge for working life, social life and personal fulfilment?

Student-teacher Relationships

Relationships between teachers and learners lie at the heart of any educational endeavour. Motivation and the quality of learning, it is generally agreed, depend on that. The following are key themes:

- teachers' expectations of students;
- students' expectations of teachers;
- student morale;
- student assessment and self-assessment; and
- teacher assessment and self-assessment.

All countries acknowledge the significance of the relationship between what teachers expect their students to be capable of, and what their students actually achieve. They also recognise the relationship between how teachers perceive their students, and how students in turn perceive their teachers. It is also widely recognised that teachers' expectations play a significant part in determining students' self-esteem and their capacity to learn. Student morale and student self-assessment are critical issues. The assessment of teachers by their students, although not yet a common feature of OECD countries, may be an issue for the future. Relevant questions include:

- What qualities do teachers value in their students?
- What qualities do students value in their teachers?
- How successful are teachers in meeting these student criteria?
- How successful are students in meeting their teachers' expectations of them?
- Do students believe that their teachers are interested in them as individuals, have faith in their abilities, are concerned about their welfare, will take time to help them with their difficulties, and will treat them with respect and fairness?

Communications

There is a cluster of issues related to the way in which schools communicate with the community and with parents. These include:

- communication of information about goals and priorities;
- communication with other professional groups;
- mechanisms and procedures for consulting with parents; and
- reporting to parents on students' achievements.

Schools everywhere are required to communicate with the outside world about what they are doing and how successful they are. Historically, they have not been very good at this nor seen it as very necessary, but schools have to become progressively more aware of the need for public relations. If international performance indicators become a reality, schools will certainly need to pay close attention to communication. Indicators of individual school performances are increasingly common in Member countries, and international indicators may further serve to make schools more aware of their clientele and their accountability to them.

Schools in all countries report to parents about student achievement, although they go about it in different ways. How successfully they do this is most important for parents since it is one of their few avenues of contact with the school. Procedures for consultation between parents and teachers (whether at school, at home or in the community) also vary but are underpinned by common concerns. These include questions such as:

- What is the level of public awareness of schools' policies and priorities?
- What is the level of awareness among employers of schools' policies and priorities?
- What is the parental view of how effectively the school provides them with information?
- What is the employers' view of how effectively the school provides them with information?

- What are the parents' attitudes to schools' reporting of student progress and achievement. For example, is it frequent enough, is it accurate enough, and does it provide parents with what they want to know?

Equality and Equity

Concerns about inequality, discrimination, and equal opportunities are common to all education systems, and have been particularly high on the international agenda in the last decade. They include the following:
- discrimination by race, sex and class;
- equal opportunities, fairness and justice;
- equality of treatment by teachers;
- provision for the disabled and students with special educational needs; and
- language and mother tongue maintenance.

All education systems have experienced immigration and find themselves in a fluid, multi-racial and multi-lingual context. Issues in equality of opportunity, the appropriateness of education in the light of varying student interests and abilities, and concern with the distribution of student achievement and attainment, have received sharply increased attention. Gender issues have in the last ten years been given a much higher social and political profile which has, in turn, been reflected in education policy. Similarly, awareness of the needs of the disabled, and other previously "invisible" groups of young people, has grown.

Students' own acute sensitivity to unequal treatment and unfairness on the part of their teachers is an age-old issue, but receptivity to the student point of view has increased in the last decade, and is concerned with common questions such as:
- Do students perceive their opportunities to be restricted by their status as members of a particular group (*e.g.* female, black, disabled)?
- Do students perceive their opportunities to be restricted by their language, dialect, or mother tongue?
- Do students feel that they are treated fairly and with justice by schools and by teachers?
- Do students feel that they are fairly treated by their peers?
- Do students feel that schools are vigilant about equality in student-student relationships?
- What are the attitudes to the provision of mother tongue teaching among the public, parents, teachers, and students?
- How are equal opportunities policies viewed by different groups? Are they seen as effective?

Education Policy

Education policies are, in all countries, shifting and developing, in part due to international pressures, very often reflecting world-wide economic, environmental and political trends. There are a number of common concerns about these embracing questions of policy. They are concerned with:

- purposes and priorities of the system;
- educational spending;
- choice and alternative schools; and
- alternative certification.

In all countries, education is in a contest for spending against other national priorities – health, the environment, social services, transport or roads, for example. How education fares in that contest differs, as do public attitudes to the priority that should be given to educational spending. Priorities for spending within the education system itself are also a common concern (teachers' salaries, buildings, or resources, for example). How priorities are perceived rests on what people see as the purposes, although the emphasis shifts from time to time. How well those purposes are communicated to the public, parents, and teachers will vary from country to country. There is also internal debate within schools about spending priorities and this will grow as schools in many countries move towards self-management. The degree of choice for students and parents within the system, and the debate over choice, are also common themes. This includes choice between state and private sectors, and choice within the mainstream system.

These different clusters of concern, brought together under the heading of "education policy", lead to the following questions:

- What are seen as the purposes of the education system?
- What level of agreement exists about those purposes?
- What are seen as the priorities of the education system?
- What level of agreement exists about those priorities?
- How effective is the system perceived to be in achieving its purposes?
- Is the public in favour of more spending on education? In relation to what other priorities?
- Is choice seen as adequate and fair?
- For what reasons do parents opt out of the public system into the private sector?

3.   An Agenda for the Future

These seven areas of common concern presented the network with an ambitious agenda for its future work. There have been opportunities to look closely at the implications of the *Common Concerns* document (MacBeath, 1991) and to cost what could be achieved. Member countries agreed that it would be prudent to start small on a trial basis. The first step, a survey of the general public, has shown the way, providing clear pointers for where the network should be going next.

A Conceptual Framework: The Rationale for Attitude Indicators
Un cadre théorique : la justification des indicateurs d'attitude

by

Alain Michel
Ministry of National Education, Paris, France

and

John MacBeath
University of Strathclyde, Scotland

People in OECD countries are becoming increasingly familiar with the idea of indicators, and, for the general public economic indicators are understood, however crudely, as providing information about the health of the economy. The building of indicators in the field of education is a more recent phenomenon. However, it can be argued that without the views of the main players – teachers, pupils, and parents – it is impossible to gauge the human qualities of schools. That desire for attitude indicators, it is argued, also has to take account of a perceived crisis in confidence in the education system and the need to give credence to public concerns, however imperfect the measures to identify them. The historical absence of indicators of opinion or attitude is explored in this chapter and difficulties of model building discussed. The problematic notion of attitudes and the assumptions on which such a notion rests is a factor to be borne in mind when drawing up indicators in this domain, and consideration has to be given to whether they are to be treated as context, process, or outcome indicators. Finally, consideration is given to the relationship with other indicators and the very future of the network structure itself.

*

*   *

Note de synthèse

Ce chapitre examine les raisons d'utiliser des indicateurs d'attitude et d'espérance. Il commence par expliquer les échecs antérieurs (en 1970), à savoir le fait qu'un soutien n'a pu être obtenu des autorités et que les préoccupations des décideurs n'ont pas été prises suffisamment en compte. L'évolution du contexte dans les années 90 a suscité une exigence de transparence et de responsabilisation, d'autant plus que beaucoup de pays ont commencé à se décentraliser.

Il a été reconnu que la série d'indicateurs devait être établie à partir du mode de fonctionnement du système et des principaux facteurs intervenant dans ce système. Puisque cette série d'indicateurs en est à un stade peu avancé d'élaboration, elle doit avoir un caractère provisoire et évolutif. Le modèle disponible le plus utile est le modèle d'entrées/sorties reposant sur trois sous-séries principales d'indicateurs – contexte de l'éducation; ressources, coûts et procédures; résultats. En suivant ce modèle théorique relativement simple, on a établi une série d'indicateurs d'attitudes et d'espérances.

Il n'existe dans aucun autre secteur de l'économie des exemples d'indicateurs fondés sur le point de vue des principaux protagonistes, mais on observe à cet égard des précédents intéressants en France et en Écosse par exemple. Toutefois, aucun pays ne s'est encore efforcé sérieusement d'établir des indicateurs systématiques réguliers fondés sur les attitudes. Il est encore plus problématique de créer un tel système dans un contexte international car cela implique que l'on se mette d'accord sur la formulation d'éléments, sur la traduction et sur la maîtrise de l'exécution et de l'analyse.

Le Réseau D a vu là un problème qui méritait d'être examiné, ses membres considérant en effet que les données quantitatives existantes étaient insuffisantes pour décrire la complexité du processus éducatif ou ses aspects « humains ». Les valeurs, les opinions et les attitudes représentent un important élément de ce processus et constituent en fait le fondement du concept de gestion totale de la qualité, et c'est sur cet élément que s'appuient les tentatives faites notamment au Royaume-Uni pour établir une « charte » des droits et responsabilités.

La « crise » de l'éducation sur laquelle des ouvrages ont été écrits dans les années 60 a pris une nouvelle forme dans les années 90, à mesure que le fossé croissant entre l'offre d'éducation et la demande sociale a suscité des doutes quant à la capacité du système éducatif à répondre aux besoins sociaux et économiques. Parallèlement, on a accordé une grande attention à la complémentarité des rôles de l'école et de la famille, à l'efficacité de l'enseignement et la gestion des écoles et aux causes d'échec ou de succès scolaire. C'est ce qui explique que bon nombre de pays aient éprouvé le besoin de déterminer le degré optimal d'autonomie de l'école.

Des problèmes épistémologiques se posent également, à savoir la définition des « attitudes » et des « espérances ». Ce ne sont ni des concepts scientifiques ni des objets rationnels, mais des sentiments subjectifs qui ne peuvent être observés. Toutefois, en tentant de les définir, on « bouleverse » la façon dont une enquête, quelle qu'elle soit, est menée. Les sondages d'opinion ont constamment démontré ce phénomène mais, bien que l'opinion publique soit capricieuse, il est possible de rendre les résultats obtenus moins

36

instables en formulant minutieusement les questions, la méthodologie, les échantillon-
nages, et les techniques d'interprétation et en examinant les tendances et les évolutions
dans le temps.

La signification à accorder à une enquête internationale dans ce domaine relève
finalement d'un jugement de valeur de nature aussi bien politique que technique. Ce
risque d'ambiguïté dans l'interprétation doit cependant être minimisé. On y parvient en
partie en plaçant les indicateurs du Réseau D dans le contexte de l'ensemble de la série
décrite dans Regards sur l'éducation. *Mais dans ce contexte, les indicateurs produits par*
le Réseau D sont-ils des indicateurs de contexte, de processus ou de résultats ? Par
certains côtés, ils sont tout cela à la fois. Ils sont le produit d'un contexte culturel et
historique et ils font partie de l'interaction dynamique entre les protagonistes scolaires et
extra-scolaires. Ce sont également des résultats qui dépendent de la façon dont le
système fonctionne dans le temps. La satisfaction du public constitue en un sens un
baromètre de l'efficacité du système.

Il est donc également important de disposer de données ventilées. Parmi les nom-
breuses possibilités théoriques de ventilation, il faut se mettre d'accord sur celles qui
sont le mieux adaptées à un contexte international et celles qui seront probablement les
plus riches d'enseignements du point de vue du contexte, du processus et des résultats. Il
doit également y avoir une coordination entre les données du Réseau D et celles des
Réseaux A et C qui utilisent également des questionnaires destinés aux élèves et aux
enseignants.

*

*   *

1.   Some Major Features of the INES Set of Indicators

The attempt to define an international set of education indicators is a new approach, taking into account the failure of the first OECD experience at the beginning of the 1970s. That project failed mainly because it did not succeed in enlisting the support of the public authorities for whom the management of resource inputs rather than educational processes and their outcomes was the key concern. Nor did it take sufficient account of the relationship between information needed to support indicators on the one hand, and issues of concern to policy-makers, on the other (Bottani and Tuijnman, 1994). The rationale for the new initiative, the INES project started in 1987, was to serve education policy, and was intended to keep the policy-makers' concerns clearly in view.

However, the definition and selection of a set of indicators cannot be either exclu-sively empirical, or determined by the main policy concerns that prevail at any given time. In order to provide relevant information for policy-makers, the indicators must draw on a realistic analysis of how the education system actually functions, as well as a theoretical framework. In other words, they must contribute to an understanding of the main factors and variables involved in the education process.

But, as the education system is a very complex one, it is difficult, or impossible, to formalise it by building a model which can adequately take account of all its various aspects. Moreover, there is no agreement yet among educational theorists on a common paradigm. Therefore, the theoretical framework upon which one can define a set of indicators has to be incomplete and evolving, that is, able gradually to integrate new findings from research in education.

Currently, the most useful model on which to build a consensus is the input/output model. This can be enriched over time with new variables, in particular those which are concerned with what is happening inside the ''black box'', in other words, ''educational processes''. This model is currently used most in analysing effectiveness and in building indicator systems, and it is the model which underpins the present set of INES indicators. There are three main sub-sets of indicators:

- the context of education;
- resources, costs and processes; and
- outputs or results.

Such a conceptual framework makes it difficult to locate any given indicator in one of these three subsets. Moreover, because the network structure reflects this sequence, it can be difficult to decide which network forum might be the most appropriate for the development of certain indicators. Are human resources, for example, an input, or are they part of the process? Is promotion through the system and eventual graduation from school a result of, or a part of, the internal processes of the system? Such questions are even less easy to answer when we enter the realm of attitudes and expectations, which is the function of Network D. Given the complexity of the education system and the controversies which surround educational theories, it was decided to build up a set of indicators consistent with a relatively simple theoretical model. This would meet two main social demands:

- the need for more transparency and objective information to inform the public debate about education (a domain in which nearly everyone feels that he or she is an expert, and to which people bring their personal prejudices); and
- the need for more rigorous information for monitoring of the education system at different levels of decision-making. This is especially relevant as countries move more or less slowly towards decentralisation in a fast-changing world which requires new cybernetic instruments and monitoring procedures (Michel, 1993). It is in this context that the introduction of indicators of attitudes and expectations is especially significant.

2. Why Introduce Indicators of Attitudes and Expectations?

Building up indicators of the attitudes and expectations of the actors in the education process is an important innovation. It does not have parallels in other domains such as the economy, where the tradition of indicators is much older. Within countries it is relatively rare. In France, for instance, the project to include a regular set of indicators of opinions among the general public, students, and teachers ("Un baromètre de l'opinion sur l'éducation"), although formulated in 1987/88, was never implemented. It has only been partly realised in the form of regular surveys of representative samples of teachers and headteachers. In Scotland, the introduction in 1992 of an innovative set of ethos indicators, designed to help schools to get at the views and expectations of parents, pupils and teachers, has been implemented at school level (HM Inspectors of Schools, 1992). A national network of schools and education authorities has been established to share good practice in Scottish schools.

There are many reasons that might explain the general absence of such indicators:
- the cost of the regular surveys needed for regular data;
- the methodological difficulties of devising questionnaires which are formulated in as neutral a way as possible;
- the methodological difficulties of extracting a few relevant indicators from results of these surveys; and
- the lack of enthusiasm of policy-makers for such regular surveys, which do not always produce welcome feedback.

As a consequence, there has not been any sustained support from politicians or researchers for indicators based on attitudes, that is, not until the recent development of the accountability movement which, as far as education is concerned, started in the 1980s. In the United States, the publication of the report *A Nation at Risk* (US National Commission on Excellence, 1983) gave a major impetus to this movement.

The difficulty of building up indicators of public attitudes is even more acute at an international level. There has to be agreement about the questionnaires to be used, the questions to be included, the formulation and translation of items, the methods of implementing surveys, the analysis of results, and the selection of the key indicators from the range of possible contenders. The desire for international attitude indicators seems, therefore, almost an impossible idea to translate into practice. For the network, it meant starting virtually with a blank sheet.

Despite these difficulties, the network was united in its view that indicators of attitude could be particularly useful in the domain of education. The collection of information about the "human" aspects of the education process is precisely because formalised models and quantitative data are insufficient to explain the complexity of the process. Given the "human" nature of this process, no-one could aim for purely scientific accuracy, but the enterprise does serve the main goal of giving more information about the context, process and outcomes of education that can be provided by minimal statistical data. It has also to be borne in mind that behaviour, attitudes, values and opinions are in fact a major element of how the education system actually works, and that the effectiveness of the system rests on people's motivation, satisfaction and sense of commitment. In moving towards more sensitive measures of "value-added" the relevance of attitudes and expectations increases, whether these are external (for example, those of parents, the general public and employers) or internal to schools (for example, those of students and teachers).

These considerations underlie the concept of total quality management. The search for quality demands that we are more conversant with the expectations and satisfaction of everyone who has a stake in the education system – and this is also a basic principle of democracy. Taking into account the expectations of clients is one of the essentials of ensuring quality; it is exemplified in the United Kingdom by "The Parents' Charter", which is based on what are seen as the rights and expectations of clients as well as their responsibilities. An information system on attitudes and expectations will be even more useful at an international level, as it will allow relative diagnostic assessments, and will help to explain differences in goals. In addition, it will inform policy-makers and the public about the functioning and outcomes of education systems in different OECD countries (Ballion, 1991).

The value of indicators of attitudes and expectations becomes even more apparent in the context of a perceived crisis in education. Much has been written on the subject in the late 1960s, and while it is a view that may be seen in some quarters as outdated, its continuing relevance can be demonstrated in objective terms. The increasing gap between educational supply and social demand has led to a crisis of confidence in the capacity of the education system to keep up with and adequately meet social and economic needs. This has led to many reforms and much discussion among OECD countries about curricular standards and the skills which are most appropriate for preparing a rising generation to enter the 21st century (OECD, 1992, 1993). An issue of widespread concern is the complementarity of roles between schools and other educational agencies, especially the family. The role and social status of teachers, the most effective teaching practices, and approaches to management, are consistently researched and reviewed in order to establish causal relationships with school success or failure. The optimal level of school autonomy and devolution of decision-making is a priority issue in virtually all OECD countries.

3. Some Questions of Definition

The first issue is the definition of "attitudes" and "expectations". These, it is argued, are "notions" rather than scientific concepts (Schubauer-Leoni, 1991). In a review of social science literature, we found more than thirty definitions of "attitude". There is no clear criterion for distinguishing "attitude" from other related notions such as representation, opinion or perception, except for one feature. Attitude implies not only an affective dimension (positive or negative feelings of indifference) and a cognitive one (positive or negative judgement or ignorance) but also a conative dimension. That is, "attitude" subsumes intended behaviour or action, whether preference for the status quo or for a change in one way or another. The same dimensions apply to the notion of "expectation".

Attitudes and expectations are subjective opinions and feelings which cannot be observed directly. One can only presume some of their characteristics from observation of behaviour, from interviews, questionnaires and so on. This epistemological problem is not specific to the social sciences. In a way, a scientific object is always built up and the real world is revealed through artefacts and models. Nonetheless, the perturbation caused by observation is particularly strong in the field of attitudes and expectations. As many researchers have shown, the results of surveys are strongly dependent on many factors, among which are:

- the formulation of the questions so as to avoid biasing the answers;
- the period of time when the questionnaire is implemented;
- the sampling procedure;
- the actual methodology of the survey; and
- the analysis of the results and their interpretation.

The risks of perturbation can be reduced through the adoption of strict methodological rules, but the results of a survey must always be interpreted with caution. As the political polls show, public opinion is, to some variable extent, capricious. Its degree of versatility, however, is not independent of the nature of the survey questions. For example, questions related to the goals of education should induce more stable answers over time than questions about the effectiveness of schools, for subjective and objective reasons.

Aggregated results should usually be more stable over time than individual results. As is the case for other data or statistics, evolution over time is a more meaningful measure. However, "external effects" are important in terms of public opinion, partly because of the influence of the mass media. It is therefore necessary to be careful in interpreting the results of a single survey. It is also useful to consider survey results as meaningful in terms of orders of magnitude, and when interpreting them to take into account all the context factors which might have influenced them (for instance, a period of particularly important social unrest).

4.   From Survey Results to Indicators

These conceptual issues were debated and worked through in the network as it sought to realise its brief of producing a set of valid indicators. That process is described more fully in Chapters 2 and 5, and in the network's Technical Report, but it is worth reminding ourselves of the delicacy of progress that is required when threading a pathway through a minefield. To the one side, there are conceptual issues; and to the other technical and methodological constraints; behind, the historical inertia determining what is and is not possible; and, in front, the political expectations of the prospective consumers of the information.

What emerges from a common international survey should lead to comparative description and analysis and to a better understanding of similarities and differences among education systems. Both the descriptive and analytical aspects are important but they have complementary purposes and address different audiences (Bradburn and Gilford, 1990).

Within the INES context, the descriptive and synthetic dimension is mainly concerned with the set of indicators to be included in *Education at a Glance* (OECD, 1995), which is intended for policy-makers and the general public. The analytical aspect (dealt with in Network D's Technical Report) is mainly of concern to the specialists in educational research. This distinction is important. However, the choice and the meaning of the indicators of *Education at a Glance* are not independent of an analysis of the data nor of some theoretical assumptions about the data which it is most important to select.

This is not, however, a simple or once-and-for-all decision because it depends on three things – the domain under consideration, the nature and pattern of the results, and the perceptions of individual countries about what is a just or fair way of representing outcomes. What, in relation to any given set of outcomes, is ''relevant'' is ultimately a matter of value judgement, and not just of a technical but of a political nature too. All these bear upon the way in which indicators are drawn up.

There is also the risk of overestimating the consensus within each country by considering only aggregate or average data (Schubauer-Leoni, 1992). Even at an international level it is of some interest to know to what degree there is agreement in different countries about important educational issues, for example, the goals of the curriculum or the importance of different subjects within the curriculum. Disaggregation therefore becomes an issue. But it is also an issue which is far from straightforward: not only is there a wide potential array of breakouts which might be used, but there is a debate between countries on which are the most telling or relevant in an international context. There is also the issue of the relationship between Network D indicators and those of other networks. Even at the mainly descriptive level it may be relevant to show significant relationships between attitude and expectation indicators, on the one hand, and indicators such as process and outcome, on the other.

They are, of course, part of the *context* since they reflect the general psychological and sociological setting in which the education system operates, and explain to a certain extent earlier political choices, specific structures, or economic and demographic factors. In other words, indicators of attitudes and expectations may be regarded both as falling under the heading of context, if they are treated primarily as ''an influence of the past'', and as reflecting the present state of the education system. Obviously, this dimension is important, as expectations and attitudes do have some stability over time. They are related to a cultural and historical background. They are not the result of spontaneous generation.

Equally, though, attitudes and expectations are a part of the education *process,* which is basically a dynamic interaction between actors inside and outside the school. While behaviour is determined by expectations, and by attitudes, it is also influenced by policies and strategies, and by representations, which are part of the discourse. Attitudes and expectations can thus be regarded as part of the process if they are considered primarily as ''currently influencing'' the functioning of the education system.

They can also be considered as *outcomes*. Attitudes and expectations are dependent on the way the education system has been functioning over time. They depend on its past and they are a result of its past. Moreover, one could argue that the level of satisfaction of the general public (for which we might read ''society'') is one important way of evaluating how effective the education system is. Attitudes and expectations may therefore be seen as an aspect of outcomes if they are considered primarily as "the results of the past and of the current functioning of the education system". Considered in this way, attitudes and expectations have a static or synchronic dimension, whereas the previous two ways of looking at indicators saw them as diachronic. When considered as part of the context, they are structural parameters. When they are seen as part of the process, they are real variables with an active role.

The relative importance of these three dimensions of indicators of attitudes and expectations may differ according to the target population of the survey. An important feature of that target population is its "exteriority". For instance, it is easier to see attitudes and expectations of the general public as part of the context than it would be to see students or teachers in that way, since they are at the very core of the education process itself.

For these reasons, it will be important to examine carefully the articulation between Network D indicators and Networks A and C, which employ background questionnaires for students and teachers. It is likely that, when trying to observe and analyse further what is actually occurring within school, class or home, Networks A and C will build up surveys also concerned with attitudes and expectations. This is likely to mean redefining the task of networks as well as redefining the typology of indicators. In the end, this may well produce a redefinition of the underlying input/output model itself.

The Policy Context: A Summary
Résumé du contexte de politique générale

by

Laura Salganik and **Lillian King**
Pelavin Research Institute, Washington DC, United States

Throughout the life of the network it has been imperative to remain attentive to questions raised by policy-makers. The survey was initiated at a time when major changes in education policy were being discussed in Member countries engaged in substantial modifications to the structure, or to parts of, the education system. A common element has been the opening up of the system to a wider array of voices, including those of parents and the general public. The development and publication of indicators have, in all countries, extensive implications for political decision-making and are, in turn, constrained and guided by policy priorities. There are both national and international policy contexts, and for network members there has to be a growing understanding not just of one's national policy framework but also of those of other countries and of the international OECD community. This chapter presents a broad overview of major issues in education and training policy for the 1990s.

*

* *

Note de synthèse

L'enquête du Réseau D a été réalisée à un moment où, dans beaucoup de pays, des changements profonds intervenaient dans le domaine de l'éducation. Presque tous ces pays avaient pour politique de faire mieux comprendre les enjeux aux parents et au public. Le chapitre 4 relie les problèmes examinés dans l'enquête aux priorités de politique générale fixées dans les pays relevant du Réseau D.

Le renforcement de l'autonomie des écoles au niveau de la prise de décisions est une question d'intérêt majeur au niveau aussi bien des programmes que du contrôle budgétaire ou de la sélection du personnel. On observe de nombreuses caractéristiques communes aux différents pays, par exemple l'existence de conseils ou commissions scolaires qui participent davantage à l'élaboration de la politique et comprennent des parents et/ou des représentants élus de la collectivité locale. Dans certains pays où le programme scolaire est fixé par l'État, les écoles disposent maintenant d'une plus grande latitude pour décider du contenu de leur enseignement ou des méthodes employées.

En même temps, on observe dans des pays traditionnellement décentralisés une évolution dans le sens de l'adoption d'un programme national et de normes nationales. Plutôt que de fixer par voie législative le contenu d'un programme pour une école, on peut fixer des normes pour diriger au niveau local le processus d'établissement des programmes, dans certains cas avec un organisme national chargé de contrôler les normes d'enseignement ou d'homologation des connaissances.

L'inclusion de cours recoupant divers programmes, de questions d'actualité, et de cours d'éducation sexuelle et environnementale par exemple, est le fait de nombreux pays qui définissent un programme de base, en supprimant certains sujets traditionnels et en en ajoutant de nouveaux.

La réforme de l'éducation influe sur le rôle et le statut des enseignants, du point de vue non seulement de l'enseignement qu'ils dispensent, mais aussi de leur image auprès du grand public. Des efforts particuliers ont été déployés pour améliorer l'image des enseignants, revaloriser leur statut grâce à une meilleure formation et homologation plus rigoureuse, en leur offrant davantage de responsabilités au sein de l'école ou en renfor-çant leur influence sur le processus de décisions.

Au premier rang du programme d'action des pays du Réseau D figure la question de la qualité de l'enseignement. Certains pays ont annoncé publiquement leur intention d'améliorer les normes et se sont fixés des objectifs. C'est ainsi que les États-Unis, tout comme la France, se proposent de faire en sorte qu'une grande majorité de la population atteigne un niveau scolaire minimum avant l'an 2000. Là où le contrôle de la qualité a été assuré par un système d'inspections, la fonction de l'inspection a changé et celle-ci sert à contrôler la réalisation d'objectifs nationaux, ou bien on permet à un public plus large d'accéder plus facilement aux conclusions des inspecteurs, comme c'est le cas au Royaume-Uni.

Ce contrôle extérieur peut être distinct d'une évaluation interne ou combiné à celle-ci. C'est ainsi qu'en Finlande et au Danemark, il n'existe pas de supervision nationale mais les écoles sont encouragées à pratiquer l'auto-évaluation, à se fixer des objectifs et à établir des plans de développement. Dans certains pays, les écoles bénéficient en outre d'une aide au niveau national sous la forme du financement d'initiatives précises, de la nomination d'experts dans de nouveaux domaines d'activité et de la fourniture de nouveaux moyens technologiques. Promouvoir la créativité et l'innovation au niveau des écoles, tel est le fondement d'une grande partie de ces approches de la réforme.

1. Placing the Survey in the Context of Policy Activity

The Network D survey comes at a time when major changes in education policy are being discussed in Member countries. In some countries, all-embracing educational reform packages, entailing major changes in the basic structure of the education system, are in the process of being implemented. In others, proposed changes have been less far-reaching, but still involve substantial modifications to parts of the system. A common element in much of the recent policy debate has been the desire to increase access to the system for a broader range of interests, including parents and the general public. The decision of Network D to conduct a survey of the public and to ground it in issues of common concern reflects this policy environment.

Four major areas of policy discussion represented in the Network D survey are: school autonomy; curriculum; the role and status of teachers; and the quality of the education system. This chapter provides examples of recent policy actions in each of these areas and is based on policy statements submitted by Member countries' representatives (the statements can be found in Bosker, 1995). The examples are illustrative rather than comprehensive, and are intended to place the survey in the context of policy activity in the participating countries.

2. School Autonomy

Increasing the decision-making authority of schools is an education policy topic of major interest in Member countries. Within the past few years, authorities in both centralised and decentralised systems, have established new arrangements that provide for increased decision-making at the school level. As a result, many countries are currently re-examining their organisational structures, and new arrangements for governing school systems that provide for increased decision-making below the national level are being implemented. Some of the areas in which schools are moving to greater autonomy include curriculum development, budgetary authority, personnel selection/setting of criteria for hiring staff, and class size.

A familiar institution among countries seeking autonomy for schools is the local school council, although the participants involved in the councils and their powers of decision-making vary. In 1985, legislation in Spain, for example, recognised the rights of communities to participate in the operation of public schools and to set up school councils comprising teachers, administrators, parents, pupils, ancillary school staff, and members of the town council. One of their responsibilities is to elect the headteacher. In Belgium (Flemish Community), there has been local participation in school councils since 1991; policy proposals currently under consideration in the Netherlands will allow for the organisation of boards and so increase parent participation in school policy development.

Schools in many countries have been given greater control over their budgets. In Portugal, schools have the right to prepare budget proposals, manage accounts, and raise their own (supplementary) funds. In individual Austrian schools, the amount of funds over which they have control was increased tenfold in a 1993 reorganisation of school autonomy. In the United Kingdom (England and Wales), a policy on local management of schools (LMS) has been adopted. Similar policy initiatives are taking place in Scotland, known there as devolved school management (or DSM).

The situation in the UK illustrates how this principle may be taken further. These schools may opt out of local authority control and become self-governing and receive a grant directly from national government. The governors within a school can vote to become self-governing, and parents can call for a vote if a significant number of them sign a written request to do so. A considerable number of schools in England have chosen this route.

In countries where the curriculum is set by the state, local decision-making power has been increased in recent years by extending schools' freedom to decide on teaching and learning methods, and, less often, on what subjects are taught. The School Reorganisation Act (1993) in Austria, for example, allows schools to determine the number of lessons to be taught in the compulsory subjects, to introduce new compulsory subjects, and to combine compulsory subjects. Schools in Belgium (Flemish Community), Denmark, France, Spain and Sweden are allowed to adapt the centrally determined curriculum to fit the needs of the students. In Finland, the education system is changing from a relatively centrally controlled system to one in which financial and curricular decisions are made (within a wide framework) at municipal and, sometimes, school levels.

3. Curriculum

What students are taught is at the heart of schooling, and major curriculum reforms in secondary education have been initiated or are under consideration in many countries. One recent trend is for countries with centralised school systems to allow increased regional or local input in the area of curriculum. For example, in Spain, 35 to 45 per cent of the new national compulsory curriculum is determined by the "autonomous communities", and the adaptation of the compulsory curriculum to the needs of particular schools is carried out by the school's teaching staff. In Sweden, a much-debated national curriculum has recently been introduced, but there is limited central regulation in the development of subject matter content and, as in Spain, schools have the freedom to organise learning to suit local conditions.

At the same time, countries with decentralised systems are seeking increased national-level input. But rather than introducing a mandatory curriculum, several countries with more decentralised school systems are debating and adopting national standards. These standards provide the state with a way to influence what students are taught while allowing individual localities to develop their own curricula. In the United States, the National Council of Teachers of Mathematics (NCTM) has published standards which are now widely used to guide mathematics curriculum development, and teachers' associations in other subject areas are at various stages in the process of developing standards. Some of these efforts are being supported financially by the federal government, which has also established a council to certify curriculum standards, although the certification process and the adoption of standards will be voluntary.

Many countries are modifying their curricula to reflect the needs of a changing world. Such modification includes incorporating contemporary subjects into the curriculum, either directly as individual courses or as cross-curricular topics. The environment has been targeted by many countries as a desirable subject. For example, in Belgium (Flemish Community), environmental education is to become a subject of study for all secondary education students in 1996 and is already a topic for cross-curricular study in Spanish schools. In the 1993/94 school year technology became a part of the core curriculum in the Netherlands. A combined subject – nature/technology – is to be introduced into the Danish curriculum in the near future. Other aspects of curriculum reform in some countries are the inclusion of sex education as a requirement, and the changing of religious education from a compulsory subject to an elective one.

4. Role and Status of Teachers

Educational reform affects teachers as well as students, and in several countries there is an on-going battle to dispel a distinctly "negative" image of teachers. In Belgium (Flemish Community), officials have recognised that both a re-evaluation of the status of the teaching profession and reforms to improve the education of teachers are needed to improve public perception of the profession. A similar situation exists in Portugal, where recent initiatives to improve teacher training and increase teachers' responsibilities have improved the status of teachers in the country. For many countries, actions taken to change the image of teachers so that they are seen as "professionals" stem from a belief that doing so will increase public support and respect for the occupation which, in turn, will boost teachers' morale and lead to improved learning and teaching.

Efforts to increase professionalisation have many forms, one of which is improving teacher education. In Austria and the United States, there is a movement to increase the stringency of teacher certification criteria and accreditation standards for teacher training programmes. Many countries, including the United Kingdom, are also providing teachers with the opportunity to update their skills and to enhance their careers by means of national and local in-service training provision. Austria, the Netherlands and Spain, have taken action to improve the working conditions of teachers by offering monetary remuneration to teachers who complete a certain amount of in-service training. In Switzerland, policy emphasises not only the importance of continuing education and enhancing of teaching skills, but also of adapting teacher training to the goals and expectations of the schools themselves.

Professionalising the role of teachers has also been associated with increasing their decision-making authority in schools. In Spain, for example, teachers' responsibilities in schools' decision-making processes have increased considerably. Enhancing the role of teachers in school-level decision-making has been a central element of recent restructuring reforms in the United States and in the moves to devolve management to schools in the United Kingdom.

Differentiation, a process that allows distinctions between different teaching duties and levels of responsibility, provides another means strengthening the teaching profession. In the Netherlands, the government has suggested that efforts be made to increase mobility and variation in the organisation of work during a teacher's career. In the United Kingdom, new posts have been created to reward teaching and enhance teachers' status without necessarily adding any administrative responsibilities.

5. Quality

Concern about quality of schools is at the top of the agenda in Network D countries, and is reflected in the policy debate about standards and goals. For example, an objective of France's Education Act of 1989 is to have 100 per cent of an age cohort obtain a "minimum qualification" (some sort of secondary schooling certificate) and to have 80 per cent of an age cohort take the *baccalauréat*. To achieve this goal by the target year 2000, the curriculum is being modified significantly. In the United States the recently enacted *Goals 2000: Educate America Act* aims to see 90 per cent of high-school students graduate by the year 2000. The new National Education Standards and Improvement Council will certify standards developed by professional associations and states for English language, mathematics, science, foreign languages, civics and government, economics, arts, history and geography.

In many countries where quality control has been provided by national inspectorates, the functioning of those inspectorates is changing. The Inspectorate in Belgium (Flemish Community), which was recently restructured, accomplishes quality control by assessing whether established attainment goals are realised. As part of the United Kingdom's policy of promoting openness, national Inspectorate teams now include lay members recruited from the public.

In some school systems, quality control is primarily an internal issue, with responsibility falling to the schools themselves. For example, Finland has no systematic assessment of the performance of schools at the national level. Nevertheless, the government encourages Finnish schools to undertake self-evaluations, make development plans, and set objectives. This is also the case in Denmark, where the individual schools are responsible for the quality of teaching that takes place in accordance with the aims laid down for teaching in the Danish *Folkeskole*. In the Netherlands, recent proposals call for attainment targets and the establishment of an internal quality control system, with schools providing progress reports both to the national Inspectorate and to parents. In the United Kingdom (Scotland), a quality assurance approach based on a partnership between national, local and school authorities, is leading to the creation of a "quality culture", combining independent inspection, quality assurance at local level, and school self-evaluation.

Countries are also relying on a variety of other measures to work toward assuring quality in education. In Spain, for example, the funds for in-service teacher training were recently increased, and new experts have been appointed to improve teaching areas such as physical education and the arts. In Austria, technical reports on improving the quality of schools have been submitted by a national group of educational science researchers; performance indicators, based on published criteria, are in use in the United Kingdom, where inspection reports on schools are distributed to parents as a matter of course. In Portugal, the Ministry of Education has established a set of nine measures intended to further the quality of education. These measures include promoting creativity and innovation in education, supporting initiatives by schools in teaching and learning, and supporting schools which are under-resourced.

Acknowledgement

The authors would like to thank the National Center for Education Statistics of the US Department of Education for supporting their work.

Design of the Study
Conception de l'étude

by

Roel Bosker
University of Twente, Enschede, the Netherlands

and

Roger Thomas
Social Community Planning Research, United Kingdom

Surveys of the general public, especially in an international context, pose a whole set of technical demands. The issues they present are essentially different from those in other indicator areas. Network D has brought to the task considerable expertise from leading experts in the Netherlands, Sweden, the United Kingdom and the United States and elsewhere, and has also learned much in the ground-breaking exercise of building an international database and conducting surveys in twelve countries and ten languages. This chapter describes the process of building such a database and deals with issues in design, administration and analysis of surveys. It explores some of the issues in the identification and construction of indicators in the attitudinal, as distinct from the outcome, field. It examines the limitations and possibilities of asking people what they think about educational issues, and looks at the relationship between individual perceptions and aggregated statistical statements. It ends with a technical prelude to provide the reader with some background to Chapter 6.

*

*   *

Note de synthèse

Ce chapitre décrit la conception et la réalisation de l'enquête du Réseau D et notamment l'établissement du questionnaire, les processus de recueil des données, les méthodes de sondage et la représentativité des sondages.

Pour établir les questionnaires, on s'est inspiré au départ des pratiques en vigueur dans tous les pays représentés et celles-ci ont dû être étudiées de façon approfondie lors de réunions de l'ensemble du réseau et examinées minutieusement avec des experts et décideurs dans les différents pays.

Pour définir les sujets et critères qualitatifs à inclure dans l'enquête auprès du public, il a fallu disposer d'une base commune d'éléments qui reflète les pratiques suivies tout en étant également comprises des personnes interrogées quelles qu'elles soient. Un certain nombre d'options supplémentaires ont été autorisées pour différents pays, là où l'on a estimé que ces options étaient importantes. Pour déterminer les éléments, le vocabulaire et les séries de réponses appropriées, le groupe technique a apporté une aide considérable en jouant un rôle pilote et en assurant la supervision voulue.

La traduction a dû être traitée avec le plus grand soin pour faire en sorte qu'un langage cohérent soit utilisé dans les différents pays et pour tenir compte des nuances propres à chaque culture. Une méthode de traduction a été approuvée selon le protocole de l'OCDE, à savoir une traduction de l'anglais dans la langue en question et une retraduction « à l'aveugle » vers l'anglais.

Autre considération importante : la méthode à utiliser, à savoir demander à l'intéressé de remplir un formulaire, l'interroger de vive voix ou lui poser des questions par téléphone. Chaque méthode comporte des avantages et des inconvénients, mais l'intérêt d'une procédure type pour tous les pays doit être mis en balance avec les coûts en jeu et les instruments existants utilisés par les différents pays. Finalement, diverses approches ont été suivies mais avec les conseils et la supervision d'un organisme britannique de renommée mondiale (SCPR : Social Community Planning Research).

La supervision des procédures de sondage a également revêtu une importance critique. Différentes approches ont été suivies, les deux principales étant le sondage fondé sur les probabilités et les quotas. La première est en général étroitement contrôlée au stade de l'établissement de l'échantillon, la seconde accordant davantage de latitude à l'enquêteur qui remplit des quotas selon des catégories prédéterminées. D'un point de vue technique, il en résulte qu'un degré minimum de confiance doit régner et que le biais de l'échantillonnage doit être pris en compte dans le calcul des erreurs types. Il a été décidé de traiter les échantillons de quotas comme des échantillons aléatoires en partant du principe que d'après les travaux types dans ce domaine, il apparaît en fait que les résultats des sondages fondés sur les probabilités et les quotas ont tendance à concorder dans le cas des enquêtes sur les opinions et les attitudes.

On a également utilisé diverses mesures pour optimiser la représentativité des échantillons, par exemple en repondérant les données par race, région ou revenu. Les détails sur les taux de non-réponse, les taux de non-réponse par élément de questionnaire et les informations sur les effets du type de sondage employé pays par pays sont présentés dans le tableau 5.1. La norme minimale souhaitée a été fixée à 1 000 réponses effectives. Dans un certain nombre de cas, du fait de la façon dont le sondage a été conçu, on est tombé légèrement au-dessous de ce chiffre, mais en fait, il est apparu qu'avec des tailles d'échantillons de plus de 800 réponses, les sondages étaient valables.

La gestion d'une enquête internationale est complexe. Il a fallu examiner et résoudre des problèmes liés à la comparabilité des systèmes, au vocabulaire utilisé et aux différences conceptuelles. La valeur des indicateurs présentés dans Regards sur l'éducation *(OCDE, 1995) est due à la rigueur des débats au sein du réseau, à la décision d'expérimenter l'instrument et au caractère très poussé des travaux des experts techniques.*

*

*   *

1.   Construction of the Questionnaire

In international comparative studies, considerable care has to be exercised in the choice and construction of survey instruments. Questionnaire items and pre-coded answers have to be grounded in existing practices in the participating countries, and be conceptually relevant and couched in appropriate language which will be understood by respondents irrespective of age, social class or educational background.

It was important, therefore, that the construction of the questionnaire (see Annex 2 to this volume) should take place in full meetings of the network, where all countries were represented, with representatives then taking away these drafts for fuller discussion with colleagues and relevant experts in their own countries. The complexity of this process may be illustrated by reference to curricular subjects. Could a dozen or more different countries all agree on a common list of subjects? Would they all refer to the first stage of secondary education as defined in each of those countries? Could the language used retain the common meaning, as well as the unique meaning, of that subject in its own cultural context? Would the subjects as described in the questionnaire actually be familiar to respondents in the participating countries? All of this was supported by the *Common Concerns* document (MacBeath, 1991).

This search for a common denominator meant inevitably that some subjects, important to individual countries, had to be omitted. However, arrangements to allow controls to add option subjects were agreed subject to a top limit on the number so as not to distort the length or response patterns of the questionnaire. Equally problematic was the designation of response categories (for example, "Essential", and "Very important"). It was an important part of the network's strategy to choose a response frame that would not restrict future options for data analysis but would be both discriminating and meaningful to the respondent. These discussions highlighted the possibility that the general public in different countries might use the response set differently, for example, inclining more to the

55

positive or negative boxes. Language had to be chosen to minimise this possibility. Was it better to use "Don't know" or "Not sure either way", and should that category sit in the middle of the positive to negative continuum or as a separate category outside the continuum?

2. Piloting of the Questionnaire

Once a final format had been agreed, it was decided to carry out a small-scale pilot study (van Blanken and Bosker, 1993). Some results of these pilot studies were that:
- the questionnaire seemed to work well: the validity was reasonable, respondents' understanding of the questions was in line with the network's thinking, and the reliability (in terms of test-retest) was high;
- the sequence of the items in the questionnaire might influence the answers.

The network members were satisfied that only minor adjustments needed to be made, but that a fixed format and sequence of items should be agreed upon. Optional questions would have to be strictly limited and approved.

3. Translation Issues

The network, with the advice of the INES Secretariat, agreed a general translation procedure to ensure that language used across Member countries was consistent, but, at the same time, able to capture the nuances of meaning that are embedded within a language and a culture. An item such as "Helping with difficulties in learning", for example, has to retain the notion that this question is about all children and about a priority of the whole school. Connotations with special needs, disability or special provision had to be avoided, as did words that refer to structures or types of special provision. Similarly, the response category "Essential" had to be translated with less concern for its literal equivalence than for the psychological weight it carries in different languages.

The procedure, based on OECD protocol, consisted of the following steps (for details see Bosker, 1995):
- translation of the English version into the national language;
- verification of the translation by a translator with good knowledge of educational terminology and concepts;
- "blind" translation from the national language back into English;
- moderation of the translation by the lead country;
- negotiation with countries over translation issues and adjustments of the translation to an agreed format.

The process was helped by the presence in the network of multi-lingual delegates.

4. Self-completion versus Interviewing

One of the first decisions to be made by the network was the type of approach to be used, postal self-completion, telephone, face-to-face interviews, etc. A balanced view needed to be taken; for example, while the use of professional interviewers has advantages in checking language, clarifying ambiguity and ensuring a higher response rate, it is more expensive. Also, interviewers tend to introduce another source of variability into results, particularly if they are allowed to rephrase questions in response to queries from respondents. There is a compelling reason for using interviewers when the questionnaire has a complex structure which might be baffling to respondents. In the case of the Network D survey, however, the structure was not complex. Each respondent was required to answer all questions, choosing, from several alternatives, the one which best represented his or her opinion. This does assume, of course, that respondents are sufficiently literate to understand the questions and sufficiently well-motivated to answer them carefully and to return the completed questionnaire.

The pilot study (van Blanken and Bosker, 1993) indicated that face-to-face interviews seemed to produce better response rates than self-completion and suggested that test-retest reliability is higher when there is an interviewer than when self-completion methods are used. However, this could well be balanced to some extent by interviewer effects within and across countries.

Several countries, including Sweden and the United Kingdom, opted for a self-completion method, but used a mixed-mode design to ensure a higher response rate than a simple postal questionnaire. For example, in the United Kingdom, the self-completion questionnaire was given to respondents who had already participated in a face-to-face interview, while in Sweden, sample members who did not respond to the initial postal questionnaire approach were followed up by telephone. The other ten countries all used an interview approach, but of these six used face-to-face interviewing and the other four used telephone interviewing. Telephone interviewing was used in countries where telephone ownership rates are high and where, as in the United States, sampling and other technology for carrying out telephone surveys is well developed. It was not such a realistic option in countries where these preconditions could not be satisfied.

The monitoring of the conduct of the surveys has been the responsibility of the participating institutions and their survey agencies but with guidance and advice from the lead country's technical advisers, Social Community Planning Research (SCPR), who enjoy an international reputation. The lead nation was satisfied that standards were assured by the selection of high-quality survey agencies within participating countries (who could be counted on to maintain high standards in executing the designs) together with the technical moderation, advice and overall monitoring role exercised by SCPR.

5. Survey Types

Lastly, it should be mentioned that three different survey types were used for collecting the data.

Ad hoc:	Dedicated, specially devised survey set up with the sole purpose of administering the network's questions.
Omnibus:	Syndicated survey, usually run on a commercial basis, in which question "slots" in a standard survey vehicle run on a repeating cycle are "bought" by clients wishing to obtain responses to particular sets of questions.
"Piggy-back":	Network D questions inserted as a module into an existing survey vehicle, normally run on a continuous or repeating basis. In practice, "piggy-back" arrangements involve government, rather than commercial surveys. These government surveys generally use probability sampling and deliver relatively high response rates.

6. Sampling Procedure: Target Population and Sample Frames

The survey aimed to represent the population of adult residents aged 18 and over in each participating country. This means that, in sampling terms, each member of the relevant population in each country should ideally have a chance of being selected. In practice, this cannot be achieved with 100 per cent certainty. In other words, the "sampled" population does not completely match the "target" population. This is because in any one country certain small sub-groups of the population are omitted from survey sampling frames, either because they are practically impossible to include, or because they can only be included at an additional cost which outweighs any possible bias resulting from their omission. Examples of omissions are: persons of no fixed address; residents of Spanish Morocco in the Spanish survey; residents of certain types of institutions, such as prisons and hospitals; and persons not reachable by telephone (in countries conducting telephone surveys).

The sample frames used by the participating countries fall into three main categories:

- *Address-based or telephone-based probability sampling (A-B Prob, T-B Prob):* Addresses/households/telephone numbers are pre-selected using probability sampling. Where more than one adult was associated with the address or telephone number, one is selected using a random method.
- *Population register-based probability (PR Prob):* In the Scandinavian countries (Denmark, Finland and Sweden), population registers exist from which approved agencies may draw samples for survey purposes. The registers contain records for all members of the national population, including personal information about individuals and contact addresses. Because of the availability of personal information it is usually possible to select probability samples from these population registers. These can be tightly controlled to reflect the composition of the population in a way which tends to reduce sampling variability.
- *Address-based non-probability sampling (A-B Non-prob):* This is often referred to as quota sampling. The size and structure of the target sample of adults is predetermined using sub-groups (quotas). The quota groups are typically defined

by reference to demographic variables such as age (grouped); gender; economic activity and status. It is usual practice for interviewers to be instructed to find and interview, say, so many economically inactive women aged 60 and over, so many economically active men aged 18-30, and so on. The target numbers within quotas are set to reflect the size of the relevant groups within the population.

7. Sampling Procedure: Sample Size

Sample survey results are always subject to random sampling variability, and the results which they provide must always be treated as estimates, with plus or minus margins of error attached to them. So, for example, if it is found that 50 per cent of the population regard the teaching of mathematics as important, there is a need also to know how much confidence can be placed in that figure. Before reporting a statistic, a decision has to be made about the level of confidence with regard to the sample value is within, say 3 per cent of the true population value in the validity of the statistic (for example a 95 per cent chance). With a sample size of 1 000 (a minimum recommended figure for INES surveys), and with 50 per cent of the respondents holding a particular view (50 per cent regard the teaching of mathematics as important whereas the other 50 per cent do not) and with a 95 confidence level, the true figure falls in a range between 47 and 53 per cent. This is the "confidence interval".

8. Sampling Procedure: Sample Designs

The calculation of standard errors depends crucially on the assumption that samples are selected randomly from the population, with all population members having a chance of selection. If the method used departs significantly from this assumption, the extent of random sampling error can no longer be calculated. Even more seriously, random sampling error may then be compounded by sampling bias. Probably the strongest argument for using strict random sampling is that it guarantees against bias. In practice that randomness may be undermined if there is a high rate of non-response or if the sample which does respond is skewed or distorted. The ideal is, therefore, random (probability) sampling coupled with high rates of response.

This combination is difficult to achieve in practice, and relatively expensive, and many commercial surveys substitute quota sampling methods. This form of sampling does not fully pre-select addresses and specific persons but leaves selection to the interviewer in the field. While this may be more or less tightly controlled, typically quotas will be filled by interviewing only adults who are both at home at the time of the call and willing to participate immediately (one reason for using quota sampling is to economise on time and cost by avoiding second calls). As regards response, the number of refusals to co-operate is sometimes recorded, but a true response rate cannot be known because "not-at-homes" are not counted and because of "interviewer-selection effects". This introduces a bias against inhabitants of addresses of types which interviewers avoid and against adults who are not readily accessible (for example, the busy and socially active). The extent of this bias cannot be estimated. Nevertheless, the quota samples will be treated as random samples in the remainder of this report. An argument that supports this decision can be found in the standard work on sampling of Cochran (1977, p. 136):

"A number of comparisons between the results of quota and probability samples are summarised by Stephan and McCarthy. The quota method seems likely to produce samples that are biased on characteristics such as income, education, and occupation, although it often agrees well with the probability samples on questions of opinion and attitude."

9. Sampling Procedure: Representativeness of the Samples

Although in most countries probability samples were used, there is still the possibility of response bias. The extent of this bias can be ascertained by taking one of the opinions/attitudes variables, looking at how the sample performs on this variable and comparing it with the population as a whole. Where samples were not representative, a mixture of measures was taken to optimise the representativeness of those samples. This involved, for example, re-weighting for, say, race, region or income. Because of national practices, the variables on which the representativeness checks were based differed greatly between the participating countries. Nevertheless, the post-stratification weights that were used to make the sample representative for the population all remained within reasonable range (< 3). Details on item non-response, non-response rates and design effects are presented in Table 5.1.

It should be noted that Denmark did not ask the question on the importance of technology as a subject; Switzerland asked the questions on responsibility and on respect for teachers in a way that differed too much from the agreed format; and in the United Kingdom the question on the importance of skills and knowledge which would help in continuing studies or training was excluded because it was added after the United Kingdom survey had begun.

The column containing the "item non-response" rates is based on the total percentage of respondents that missed at least one item. For social surveys of this kind these figures are, given the length of the questionnaire, reasonable. It is more problematic when the response rate does not meet the standard set (80 per cent). In all cases, however, checks were made on possible response bias and, if it occurred, post-stratification weights were constructed to adjust for this. The last column shows that although achieved sample sizes met the standard set (1 000), in some instances design effects reduced these sizes effectively to ranges below 1 000. For statistical purposes the effective sample sizes were used, and with sizes greater than 800 the power of the tests is good.

Table/Tableau 5.1.

Sample size and non-response

Taille des échantillons et non-réponses

	Item non-response (%)	Type of sample	Achieved sample size	Effective sample size
Austria	8.7	Address-based probability sample	1 757	1 757
Belgium (Flemish Community)	8.6	Address-based probability sample	1 000	808
Denmark	4.5	Population register-based probability sample	1 135	1 135
Finland	3.3	Population register-based probability sample	1 283	1 283
France	8.1	Address-based non-probability sample	1 508	1 508
Netherlands	1.1	Address-based probability sample	1 000	934
Portugal	2.8	Address-based probability sample	1 336	1 271
Spain	12.0	Address-based non-probability sample	2 500	1 399
Sweden	15.3	Population register-based probability sample	1 911	1 003
Switzerland	3.2	Address-based non-probability sample	1 000	980
United Kingdom	14.7	Address-based probability sample	1 306	1 242
United States	3.9	Telephone-based probability sample	1 281	1 281

Source: OECD, INES project.

10. Overcoming Difficulties

The management of an international survey is a complex process, and it was not embarked upon lightly by Network D. Issues of comparability of educational systems, language and conceptual differences underlying language, all had to be discussed and resolved by participating countries. There are many technical issues associated with finding the appropriate form of survey, sampling and analysis, and ultimately with the confidence one can have in the validity of the findings. The value of the data and indicators reproduced in *Education at a Glance* (OECD, 1995) is due to the rigour of the discussion within the network, the decision to pilot the instrument at an early stage, the advice and support of the INES Secretariat, and the strength of the work carried out by agencies in Member countries. The network benefited from its ability to draw on the technical expertise of its members, the intensive work of its technical sub-group, and the combined technical expertise of SCPR, the Scottish Office Analysis Unit and the University of Twente. All of this lends confidence to the reporting and interpretation of the results, dealt with in Chapters 6 and 7. Full details, including a country-by-country commentary, are given in the network's technical report (Bosker, 1995).

11. A Technical Prelude to Chapter 6

Chapter 6 which follows, reports the findings of country surveys, sometimes comparing country by country, sometimes issue by issue. It also includes an examination in more details of the overall statistics, and looks at particular groups of respondents, for example:

- male/female;
- parents of school-age children/non-parents;
- respondents by length of formal education; and
- respondents by age group.

This approach is sometimes referred to as "breakouts".

Some of these ways of defining groups are more problematic than others. *Length of formal education* is probably the most problematic because educational systems vary so much. Level of education is, therefore, translated to a common code – the International Standard Classification for Education (ISCED). For breakout purposes, respondents are divided into two categories: up to ISCED level 2 (lower secondary education); and above ISCED level 2. This poses a problem of terminology when groups are compared and, as a result, it was decided for the sake of simplicity to refer to these two groups as *early school leavers* and *late school leavers*. This information was not available for the Swiss data at the time of analysis.

Other breakouts look at the views of *male/female* populations and of *parents* and *non-parents*. Parents were defined as having "school age children", which was also a slightly ambiguous expression and differed from country to country though not enough to affect the overall patterns of information. A fourth breakout referred to in the following chapter is *age*. The age of respondents has been classified into three groups: 18-29; 30-59; and 60 plus.

Breakouts by length of formal education, parental status and age are not, of course, independent of each other. For example, parents tend to fall into the middle age group, and considerably fewer are to be found in the upper age group. The oldest age group is also likely to be over-represented in the "early leavers" category because people tended to leave school earlier 40 or 50 years ago. Females are also over-represented in the "60 plus" group simply because of their greater life expectancy than males. Some of

Table/Tableau 5.2.

Breakout information

(%)

Ventilation de l'information

	Percentage in each age-group	Up to and including ISCED level 2	Above ISCED level 2	Parents	Non-parents	Male	Female
Aged 18-29 years	24	13	32	15	29	24	23
Aged 30-59 years	39	30	45	66	24	40	38
Aged 60 or over	37	57	23	19	47	36	39
Total sample	14 600	5 601	7 869	5 238	9 289	6 926	7 641

Source: OECD, INES project.

these factors are illustrated in Table 5.2. It takes the whole sample, comprising 14 600 people, and breaks it down by the three age groups. It shows the percentage of respondents in each age group who fell into the other three main breakout categories – length of formal education, parents/non-parents, gender.

It can be seen that it has to be borne in mind when one is looking at any one group that its membership often overlaps heavily with that of another group. This is most obvious in breakouts by length of education, since 57 per cent of those at ISCED level 2 and below are aged over 60.

Breakout information is generally presented without ''Not sure'' being treated as missing data. Where it assumes some importance it is discussed in the following chapters.

Chapter/Chapitre 6

The Findings
Principaux résultats de l'enquête

by

Carol Calvert
Scottish Office Education Department, Edinburgh, Scotland

and

John MacBeath
University of Strathclyde, Scotland

This chapter sets out the main findings from the survey in Member countries. These are described in turn, following the main themes of the questionnaire – the importance of subjects, of qualities and aptitudes, the public's confidence in how well these are taught, perceptions of school priorities and autonomy, respective roles of school and home, and the perceived status of teachers, including salaries. Some of the most interesting and informative of the tables are selected, highlighting both similarities and differences between countries. Disaggregation is also dealt with wherever possible and/or relevant. The discussion does not, at this point, go into interpretation but does try to set the findings in a comparative context, pointing to some of the issues that have to be borne in mind when reading, and trying to make sense of, international data.

*

*　　*

Note de synthèse

Le chapitre 6 présente les principales conclusions de l'enquête réalisée dans douze pays. On a recueilli une moisson de données qui doivent être traitées de façon très sélective. Les questions suivantes sont analysées grâce à des tableaux et des données détaillées par pays et, le cas échéant, des ventilations par âge, sexe, ou durée de l'enseignement de type scolaire.

Importance des différentes disciplines et confiance qu'inspire leur mode d'enseignement

On a demandé au public de classer dix matières scolaires par ordre d'importance. Dans tous les pays, la langue locale et les mathématiques ont été classées parmi les disciplines les plus importantes. Les langues étrangères se sont également vu attribuer un rang constamment élevé, sauf dans les deux pays anglophones (États-Unis et Royaume-Uni). Alors que dans certains pays, on constate une hiérarchie bien définie entre les matières les plus importantes et celles qui le sont le moins, tous les pays ne font pas une distinction aussi nette. En ce qui concerne la confiance qu'inspire le mode d'enseignement des diverses disciplines, les variations sont beaucoup moins marquées d'une matière à l'autre mais la confiance globale dans l'enseignement des matières scolaires est systématiquement plus faible que le classement de celles-ci par ordre d'importance.

Importance des qualités personnelles et de la façon dont celles-ci sont renforcées à l'école

Le développement des « qualités personnelles » (par exemple, la confiance en soi, les compétences pour obtenir un emploi) se voit attribuer autant d'importance que les matières scolaires proprement dites par la population de tous les pays. Sur les huit qualités qui ont fait l'objet de l'enquête, la confiance en soi apparaît régulièrement comme celle à laquelle les répondants attachent le plus d'importance. Toutefois, en ce qui concerne la confiance dans le développement de ces qualités par l'école, le public est régulièrement plus sceptique qu'au sujet de l'enseignement des matières scolaires, bien que les personnes âgées et les parents aient tendance à avoir une opinion plus positive que les jeunes et les non-parents. Les qualités considérées comme assez bien développées par l'école sont « le désir de poursuivre des études ou de recevoir une formation » et les « compétences et connaissances qui aideront à poursuivre des études ou à recevoir une formation ».

Objectifs prioritaires de l'école

On a soumis au public sept objectifs prioritaires à assigner éventuellement à l'école en lui demandant de les classer par ordre d'importance. Dans l'ensemble, un contraste marqué a été constaté entre un objectif prioritaire et un autre, celui qui a été le plus constamment considéré comme prioritaire étant d'« aider les élèves qui ont des difficultés à apprendre ». Les différences d'un pays à l'autre ont été parfois prononcées, par exemple en ce qui concerne l'autorité du professeur principal, objectif considéré comme hautement prioritaire dans certains pays, mais pas dans d'autres. Sur la question de l'autorité, les personnes âgées ont tendance à y accorder plus d'importance, ainsi qu'au maintien de la discipline et aux devoirs réguliers à la maison, que les groupes d'âge plus jeunes. Sur ce point, les parents ont donné des réponses nettement plus positives que les non-parents.

Qui doit être responsable de l'épanouissement personnel et du développement social?

On a demandé au public si, selon lui, la responsabilité de l'épanouissement personnel et du développement social incombait davantage à la famille ou à l'école ou s'il s'agissait davantage d'une responsabilité partagée. Les réponses ont varié sensiblement d'un pays à l'autre, le public considérant dans certains pays que cette responsabilité incombait essentiellement à la famille tandis que dans d'autres pays, il insistait sur le fait qu'elle était partagée entre la famille et l'école. Aucun pays n'a considéré que cette responsabilité incombait essentiellement à l'école. Les femmes ont eu davantage tendance que les hommes à estimer qu'elle devait être partagée entre la famille et l'école. Il n'y a pas eu de différence entre la réponse des parents et des non-parents sur ce point, mais on a observé un rapport entre l'importance attribuée par le public à certaines qualités et l'accent mis sur le fait que la responsabilité de l'épanouissement personnel et du développement social est partagée entre la famille et l'école.

Processus de décision

Dans quels domaines l'école devrait-elle contrôler le processus de décision? Parmi les six domaines possibles considérés, c'est pour les méthodes d'enseignement que le public a estimé que l'école devait avoir le plus grand pouvoir de décision, son pouvoir devant au contraire être particulièrement limité en ce qui concerne les traitements et conditions de travail des enseignants. Des variations considérables ont cependant été constatées d'un pays à l'autre. Dans un même pays, on a également observé des différences sensibles selon l'âge, le sexe ou le nombre d'années d'enseignement traditionnel. Dans certains pays, les parents ont eu davantage tendance que les non-parents à accorder un grand pouvoir de décision à l'école dans les six domaines considérés sans exception, en particulier en ce qui concerne la rémunération et les conditions de travail des enseignants, et le temps consacré à l'enseignement des matières scolaires. Les personnes âgées, les femmes et les personnes ayant interrompu leurs études à un stade précoce ont été généralement plus favorables à la prise de décisions au niveau de l'école.

Respect des professeurs de l'enseignement secondaire

Les répondants ont été invités à se prononcer sur le degré général de respect qu'inspirent les enseignants. Dans tous les pays (sauf l'Espagne), ils ont estimé dans leur majorité que les enseignants étaient « très » ou « assez » respectés mais ces réponses ont différé considérablement selon le groupe social. On a observé une différence très sensible d'opinion en fonction du nombre d'années d'études, les enseignants inspirant plus de respect aux personnes ayant quitté l'école à un stade précoce. Les personnes âgées ont eu nettement plus tendance que les jeunes à considérer que les enseignants étaient respectés, de même que les parents par rapport aux non-parents, mais on n'a pas enregistré de différences sensibles entre hommes et femmes.

Rémunération des enseignants

Neuf pays seulement ont demandé au public s'il estimait que les enseignants devraient être payés plus ou moins qu'ils ne le sont actuellement. On a enregistré de grandes différences d'un pays à l'autre. C'est ainsi qu'aux États-Unis, 64 pour cent des personnes interrogées ont estimé que les enseignants devraient gagner davantage, contre 18 pour cent en Espagne. Dans tous les pays, un petit pourcentage seulement a estimé qu'ils étaient trop payés. Dans certains pays, un nombre relativement élevé de personnes n'avaient « pas d'opinion précise » à ce sujet, en particulier dans la catégorie des personnes ayant quitté l'école à un stade précoce. Lorsqu'on examine, par rapport au pouvoir d'achat, les opinions exprimées sur la question de savoir si les traitements des enseignants devraient être augmentés ou réduits, on voit apparaître des schémas complexes entre la rémunération des enseignants et le respect qu'ils inspirent.

*

*   *

1. Introduction: Points to be Borne in Mind

The primary purpose of conducting surveys in twelve countries was to generate data which could be translated into comparative indicators. The confidence which the network could have in these data as saying something valid and significant would inevitably be open to debate, but would rest on as systematic and rigorous a methodology as possible, as was acknowledged in the preceding chapter. Members recognised that the data would be rich and extensive, and that to make sense of it would be a painstaking and creative job. The analysis and presentation of these data would demand a selective judgement about the quality and value of what should be highlighted. What is presented here is *a selection from a vast array of data,* but represents, in the view of the network members, the essence of survey findings across participating countries. The prelude at the end of Chapter 5 introduced this chapter, and it is important to emphasise that the following points should be borne in mind when *reading the tables and figures*:

- In the tables and graphs, countries are given in alphabetical order unless indicated otherwise; the items (such as school subjects, for example) are arranged from left (high) to right (low).
- Standard errors have been calculated according to the country's methods of sampling. In three countries, Belgium (Flemish Community), France and Spain, an element of quota sampling was used. For these samples, standard errors have been calculated as if they were random samples, as is common practice in the field. Full

details of the way in which design effects, the weights and standard errors were calculated are given in the network's technical report (Bosker, 1995).

- The percentages given in the table are weighted to reflect the sample designs in each country. Table 5.1 in Chapter 5 indicates sample sizes and type of sampling. The combined countries figures in the tables, and those for breakouts across the whole data set, are calculated from all individual respondents' data, appropriately weighted, as opposed to being the average of the individual country figures. The weights used are the individual weights attached to each respondent combined with a weight which compensates for slightly different sample sizes in countries. This enables standard errors to be calculated and means that equal weight is given to the results from each country (the use of breakouts is considered in the technical prelude under Section 11 in Chapter 5).

The chapter has seven sub-sections corresponding broadly to the issues covered in the network's questionnaire (see Annex 2 to this volume):

- importance of different subjects, and confidence in how they are taught (Questions 1 and 2 of the questionnaire);
- importance of qualities and confidence in how they are developed in schools (Questions 3 and 4 of the questionnaire);
- priorities for schools in achieving their goals (Question 5 of the questionnaire);
- personal and social development – whose responsibility? (Question 6 of the questionnaire);
- locus of decision-making (Question 7 of the questionnaire);
- respect for secondary-school teachers (Question 8 of the questionnaire); and
- teachers' salaries (Question 9 of the questionnaire).

2. The Importance of Different Subjects and Confidence in How they are Taught

What did the general public in OECD countries see as important subjects to be taught in school? The question is relevant in an international context because assumptions may easily be made about the content of the curriculum without testing those assumptions against what happens in other countries and against what the general public have to say. A sample of the public was presented with a list of ten subjects and asked to rate them on a five-point scale from "Essential" to "Not at all important", plus a sixth category to indicate "Not sure either way". To present all the aggregated data from twelve countries would require a $10 \times 6 \times 12$ grid; a judgement has therefore to be made about what to select as relevant and significant. In Table 6.1 two response categories ("Essential" and "Very important") have been combined in order to differentiate those subjects which people felt most strongly about from those where they held positive, but less emphatic, views (standard errors are shown for each subject).

Table/Tableau 6.1.

The percentage of respondents who felt the subject was either "essential" or "very important"

Pourcentage de répondants ayant estimé que la matière était « essentielle » ou « très importante »

	Native language		Mathematics		Foreign languages		Information technology		The sciences		Social subjects		Education for citizenship		Physical education		Technology/ technical studies		The arts		Subject average
	%	S.E.	%	S.E.	%	S.E.	%	S.E.	%	S.E.	%	S.E.	%	S.E.	%	S.E.	%	S.E.	%	S.E.	%
Austria	92	0.7	92	0.7	91	0.7	79	1.0	67	1.1	72	1.1	64	1.1	73	1.1	60	1.2	43	1.2	73.2
Belgium (Flemish Com.)	86	1.2	80	1.4	88	1.2	77	1.5	57	1.7	44	1.8	66	1.7	63	1.7	53	1.8	29	1.6	64.3
Denmark	85	1.1	81	1.2	79	1.2	55	1.5	46	1.5	41	1.5	46	1.5	38	1.4	–	–	36	1.4	56.3
Finland	77	1.2	84	1.0	87	0.9	71	1.3	53	1.4	49	1.4	35	1.4	61	1.4	39	1.4	31	1.3	58.9
France	97	0.4	88	0.8	87	0.9	69	1.2	63	1.2	69	1.2	67	1.2	50	1.3	47	1.3	31	1.2	66.8
Netherlands	90	1.0	69	1.5	85	1.2	75	1.4	64	1.6	47	1.6	41	1.6	41	1.6	42	1.6	31	1.5	58.6
Portugal	91	0.8	86	1.0	85	1.0	76	1.2	76	1.2	75	1.2	73	1.3	71	1.3	66	1.3	55	1.4	75.5
Spain	67	1.3	73	1.2	72	1.2	66	1.3	65	1.3	66	1.3	70	1.5	52	1.3	63	1.3	44	1.4	63.4
Sweden	94	0.8	91	0.9	87	1.1	63	1.5	65	1.5	58	1.6	70	1.5	54	1.6	38	1.5	31	1.5	65.0
Switzerland	84	1.2	82	1.2	77	1.3	71	1.4	63	1.5	62	1.6	65	1.5	67	1.5	52	1.6	58	1.6	68.0
United Kingdom	88	0.9	93	0.7	56	1.4	72	1.3	66	1.4	50	1.4	36	1.4	41	1.4	57	1.4	26	1.2	58.4
United States	92	0.8	96	0.6	53	1.4	86	1.0	85	1.0	80	1.1	77	1.2	62	1.4	36	1.3	47	1.4	71.3
Combined countries	86.9	0.3	84.6	0.3	79.0	0.3	71.5	0.4	64.1	0.4	59.5	0.4	59.1	0.4	56.0	0.4	50.2	0.4	38.4	0.3	

Note: The above question was not asked for the subject "Technology/technical studies" in Denmark. In the Swiss questionnaire, the subject "Native language" includes the teaching of French, German and Italian. "Foreign languages" implies the teaching of English.

S.E. = Standard error.

Source: OECD, INES project.

Showing the Standard Error

The most useful starting point for interpreting Table 6.1 is the combined countries figure. It shows that native language is rated as more important than other subjects and that the arts lie at the other extreme. The standard error which accompanies the combined countries average is a reminder of the need to be cautious when comparing the public's rating of subjects. So, for example, although the combined countries figure for social subjects is higher than that for education for citizenship, the difference between the two figures lies within the bands of error associated with sample surveys. It is not possible to say that social subjects is rated higher than education for citizenship. On the other hand social subjects can be said to be rated higher than physical education, technology and the arts.

Presenting combined countries importance in the form of a graph with a standard error added, allows the significance of differences from subject to subject to be grasped more clearly. Figure 6.1 shows the combined countries figure for each subject with the shaded area at the top representing the possible margin of error.

Figure 6.1 reveals a clear ordering of most highly rated to least highly rated of subjects when data from all countries are taken together. To look for patterns of priorities *within* countries it is necessary to return to Table 6.1, from which a similar graph could be drawn for each individual country. What that would show is a level of consistency

Figure/*Graphique* 6.1. **The combined countries importance by subject**
Importance attribuée par l'ensemble des pays aux différentes matières

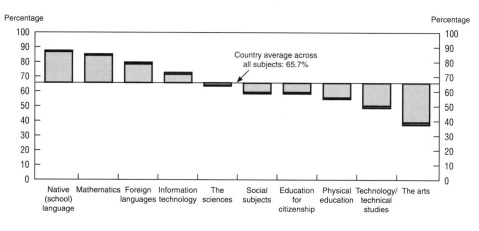

Note: The figures are for the combined "essential" and "very important" responses. The small solid black area represents the 95 per cent confidence interval, that is, there is a 95 per cent likelihood that the "true percentage" lies somewhere within the black area.
Source: OECD, INES project.

Figure/*Graphique* 6.2. **Subject averages in Finland and Spain**
Importance moyenne accordée aux différentes matières en Finlande et en Espagne

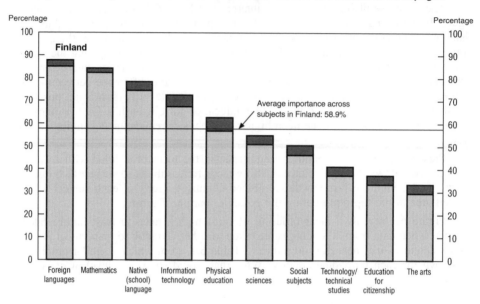

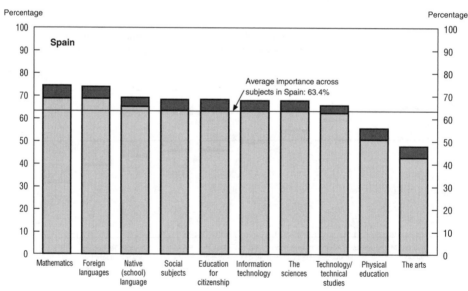

Note: The figures are for the combined "essential" and "very important" responses.
Source: OECD, INES project.

among countries in their own internal ordering, or prioritisation, of subjects. Native language and mathematics are consistently high and the arts have a consistently low rating among all countries. Variation tends to be small. For example, in Finland, foreign languages are rated highest followed by mathematics and then native languages. This is the reverse of the order of these three in the combined countries graph. Within the United Kingdom and United States, the priority given to foreign languages, by comparison with mathematics and the native languages, is significantly out of step with the other ten countries.

Looking at Individual Countries

Graphing each country individually would provide an immediate view, not simply of the ordering of priorities, but of the size of difference in rating of subjects. The example from Finland and Spain shown in Figure 6.2 illustrates some contrasting features.

Figure 6.2 reveals that there is, broadly, a consistency from most to least important subjects, but that there are quite marked differences in the gap between highest and lowest-rated subjects and in the gradations between them. In Finland, the difference between each subject is significant, but this is not the case in Spain. When standard error is taken into account, the subjects in the Spanish graph fall into four distinct groups or "blocks". Mathematics and foreign languages are of similar or equal importance and comprise priority block one. Then there is a second block comprising native language, social subjects, education for citizenship, information technology, the sciences and technology. Physical education forms a block on its own, and the arts provide the fourth and final block.

From Importance to Confidence

The network agreed that it was important to know not simply whether or not the public saw certain subjects as important, but also their level of confidence in the actual teaching of those subjects. This could be found by presenting respondents with the same list of subjects as before and asking for their judgements about how well each of these was taught. To present the aggregation of results from all countries would again require a $10 \times 6 \times 12$ grid, and again the most telling table is probably the conflation of the "Very confident" and "Fairly confident" categories country by country, as is shown in Table 6.2.

If we again examine the combined countries figures, mathematics emerges across countries as the subject which the general public are most likely to see as being taught well, but there is only a small difference between this and native language; and indeed among the top five, there is little variation. This is shown more graphically in Figure 6.3.

Again, similar profiles could be provided for each individual country and would show some marked differences *within countries*, both in terms of level of confidence and level of differentiation, or number of blocks. Figure 6.4 compares Belgium (Flemish Community) and Switzerland. Key features of the graphs are obvious at a glance:

Table/Tableau 6.2.

The percentage of respondents who felt either
"very confident" or "fairly confident" that the subject was being taught well

Pourcentage de répondants estimant «très probable» ou «assez probable» que la matière est enseignée de façon efficace

	Mathematics		Native language		The sciences		Foreign languages		Social subjects		Information technology		Physical education		Technology/ technical studies		The arts		Education for citizenship		Subject average
	%	S.E.	%	S.E.	%	S.E.	%	S.E.	%	S.E.	%	S.E.	%	S.E.	%	S.E.	%	S.E.	%	S.E.	%
Austria	87	0.8	83	0.9	79	1.0	79	1.0	78	1.0	65	1.2	72	1.1	61	1.2	69	1.1	64	1.2	73.8
Belgium (Flemish Com.)	85	1.3	84	1.3	80	1.4	78	1.5	73	1.6	66	1.7	54	1.8	67	1.7	47	1.8	42	1.7	67.6
Denmark	83	1.1	75	1.3	77	1.3	83	1.1	69	1.4	64	1.4	66	1.4	–	–	67	1.4	69	1.4	72.6
Finland	84	1.1	86	1.0	81	1.2	83	1.1	80	1.2	67	1.4	64	1.4	68	1.4	61	1.5	66	1.4	74.0
France	92	0.7	88	0.8	87	0.9	84	0.9	87	0.9	77	1.1	78	1.1	78	1.1	62	1.3	64	1.2	79.8
Netherlands	71	1.5	65	1.6	71	1.5	73	1.5	59	1.6	53	1.6	50	1.6	42	1.6	39	1.4	40	1.6	56.2
Portugal	58	1.4	59	1.4	60	1.4	61	1.4	60	1.4	47	1.4	49	1.4	46	1.4	49	1.4	41	1.4	52.9
Spain	51	1.3	50	1.3	44	1.3	40	1.3	49	1.3	34	1.3	35	1.3	32	1.3	29	1.2	33	1.3	39.7
Sweden	49	1.6	47	1.6	33	1.5	43	1.6	31	1.5	25	1.4	24	1.4	22	1.3	17	1.2	30	1.5	32.0
Switzerland	84	1.2	79	1.3	79	1.3	75	1.4	76	1.4	68	1.5	78	1.3	64	1.5	64	1.5	62	1.6	72.8
United Kingdom	65	1.4	62	1.4	66	1.4	51	1.4	63	1.4	66	1.4	64	1.4	59	1.4	50	1.4	39	1.4	58.3
United States	70	1.3	66	1.3	64	1.3	53	1.4	67	1.3	67	1.3	64	1.3	58	1.4	56	1.4	48	1.4	61.4
Combined countries	73.0	0.4	70.3	0.4	68.4	0.4	66.8	0.4	65.9	0.4	58.2	0.4	58.2	0.4	54.2	0.4	50.9	0.4	49.7	0.4	

Note: The above question was not asked for the subject "Technology/technical studies" in Denmark. In the Swiss questionnaire, the subject "Native language" includes the teaching of French, German and Italian. "Foreign languages" implies the teaching of English.

S.E. = Standard error.

Source: OECD, INES project.

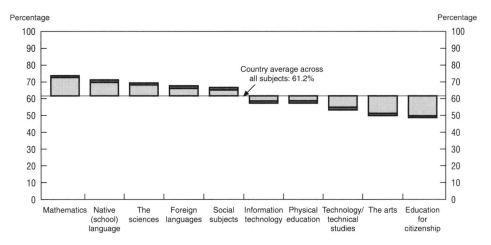

Figure/*Graphique* 6.3. **The combined countries confidence by subject**
Confiance de l'ensemble des pays dans la qualité de l'enseignement des différentes matières

Note: The figures are for the combined "very" and "fairly" confident categories.
Source : OECD, INES project.

1) confidence levels are on average lower in Belgium; 2) there is greater differentiation between one subject and another in Belgium; and 3) there are some marked differences in ordering of priorities. In Belgium, for example, confidence in the teaching of physical education is significantly lower than that in the teaching of technology/technical studies, whereas in Switzerland it is the other way around.

For the purposes of indicators, the most useful information is about people's level of confidence in what *they see as important subjects.* On the face of it, it would appear that those subjects rated as important also tended to be rated as taught well. It is not, however, quite that straightforward. For example, education for citizenship is rated overall seventh in importance but only tenth in terms of confidence. Such differences are even more sharply focused if we look at individual countries. In Austria, education for citizenship was seen to be important by 64 per cent and also taught well by 64 per cent. In Portugal, on the other hand, 73 per cent of respondents felt that it was important, but only 41 per cent saw it as being taught well. Since it is the function of indicators to raise questions, rather than to answer them, possible explanations for such findings are left to Chapter 7.

Summary

- Native language(s), foreign languages and mathematics are viewed as among the most important subjects in most countries.

Figure/*Graphique* 6.4. **Confidence in subjects in Belgium and Switzerland**
Confiance dans l'enseignement des différentes matières en Belgique et en Suisse

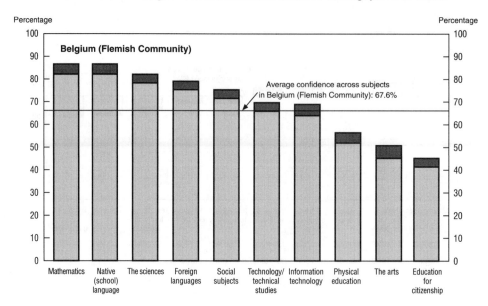

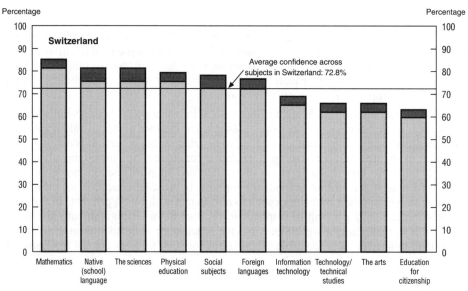

Note: The figures are for the combined "very" and "fairly" confident categories.
Source: OECD, INES project.

76

- In some countries, several subjects are viewed as equally important whilst in others a clear hierarchy of importance exists.
- There is generally less variation for confidence in the teaching of subjects than for importance of subjects.

3. The Importance of Qualities, and Confidence in How they are Developed in Schools

The views of members of the general public on the importance of subjects is influenced by their personal experience of school. For most people the timetable, with its allocation by subject, remains an indelible image. Thinking about the priorities given by schools to developing personal qualities is of a different conceptual order, however, and the responses might be expected to be different. The combined countries figures for importance of qualities, given in Figure 6.5 show, in fact, some close parallels to Figure 6.1, which depicts the ordering of subjects.

As Figure 6.5 shows, qualities are, at the top end, rated as highly as the top-ranking subjects, with the lowest-ranking quality (understanding of people in other countries) rated significantly higher than the bottom-rated subject.

Figure/*Graphique* 6.5. **The combined countries importance of qualities**
Importance des qualités attribuées à l'enseignement par les différents pays

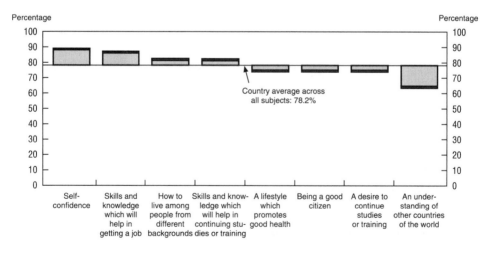

Note: The figures are for the combined "essential" and "very important" responses.
Source: OECD, INES project.

77

Table/Tableau 6.3.

Grouping of importance of qualities by country

Ensemble de qualités jugées importantes par les différents pays

	Block 1	Block 2	Block 3	Block 4	Block 5	Block 6
Austria	Self-confidence Skills – job	Skills training	Backgrounds Good health	Desire training	Other countries	Good citizen
Belgium (Flemish Community)	Self-confidence	Skills – job	Backgrounds Good citizen Good health Skills training Desire training	Other countries		
Denmark	Self-confidence	Backgrounds	Skills – job	Skills training	Desire training Good citizen Good health Other countries	
Finland	Self-confidence Backgrounds	Skills – job	Good health Skills training Good citizen	Desire training	Other countries	
France	Self-confidence	Skills – job	Desire training Good health Skills training Backgrounds Good citizen	Other countries		
Netherlands	Self-confidence	Backgrounds Skills training	Skills – job	Desire training	Good citizen Good health Other countries	
Portugal	Good citizen Good health Skills training Skills – job	Self-confidence Backgrounds Desire training	Other countries			
Spain	All except Other countries	Other countries				
Sweden	Self-confidence	Skills – job	Skills training	Good citizen Backgrounds Good health	Desire training	Other countries
Switzerland	Self-confidence	Skills – job Backgrounds Skills training	Good health Desire training Other countries	Good citizen		
United Kingdom	Skills – job	Self-confidence	Good citizen	Backgrounds Good health	Desire training	Other countries
United States	Skills – job	Skills training Self-confidence Desire training Good citizen	Good health Backgrounds	Other countries		

Note: The figures are for the combined "essential" and "very important" responses. Within a country, qualities are ordered on the combined percentage of "Essential" and "Very important" responses. The separation of one block from the next is obtained by working down the priority list and cutting-off each time any quality has a significantly different percentage from the quality above it. This then becomes the first quality in a new block. Only when the next quality with a significantly different percentage is reached is a new block formed. This means that every quality in a block is significantly different, in terms of the way it was rated, from any quality in another block (on occasions, where there are a number of items in a block there may be a significant difference between the highest and lowest rated).

Source: OECD, INES project.

Using the blocking idea, it is possible to get a country-by-country picture of high and low-rated qualities as well as the degree of "spread". The "blocks" of qualities in Table 6.3 are shown from left to right in order of importance. The development of self-confidence is regarded within every country as a high priority and falls into Block 1 in nine countries and into Block 2 in the other three. Other qualities show considerable variation. For example, the Portuguese and Spanish public give a high rating to "Being a good citizen" while the Austrian and Swiss public rate it lowest.

From Importance to Confidence

When it comes to qualities being developed well, confidence levels are generally lower than for subject teaching. In Figure 6.6, the variation of qualities from the overall average is less than was evident in Figure 6.3 for subjects. The public appear to have greatest confidence in those areas which are related to work and training, but consistently less faith when it comes to the development of self-confidence.

The picture changes slightly if we consider individual countries. Countries tend to split into fewer blocks in "confidence" ratings than in "importance" rating (see Table 6.4). In Sweden, for example, importance ratings fall into six blocks whereas confidence ratings fall into only two. In Belgium (Flemish Community) and Portugal, there are also just two confidence blocks and in Spain only one.

Figure/*Graphique* 6.6. **The combined countries confidence in qualities**
Confiance de l'ensemble des pays dans la qualité de l'enseignement

Note: The figures are for the combined "very" and "fairly" confident categories.
Source: OECD, INES project.

79

Table/Tableau 6.4.

Grouping of confidence of qualities by country

Ensemble de qualités attribuées à l'enseignement dans les différents pays

	Block 1	Block 2	Block 3	Block 4	Block 5	Block 6
Austria	Desire training	Skills training	Skills – job Other countries Backgrounds Good citizen	Self-confidence Good health		
Belgium (Flemish Community)	Desire training Skills training	Backgrounds Skills – job Self-confidence Other countries Good citizen Good health				
Denmark	Skills training Desire training	Other countries Backgrounds Skills - job Good citizen	Good health			
Finland	Skills training	Desire training	Good citizen Good health Other countries	Skills – job Backgrounds	Self-confidence	
France	Skills training Backgrounds Desire training	Other countries	Self-confidence	Good citizen Good health	Skills – job	
Netherlands	Skills training	Desire training	Other countries Background Skills – job	Self-confidence	Good citizen	Good health
Portugal	All except Skills – job	Skills – job				
Spain	All					
Sweden	Skills training	All except Skills training				
Switzerland	Desire training Skills training	Skills – job	Other countries Backgrounds	Good health Self-confidence Good citizen		
United Kingdom	Skills – job Desire training	Self-confidence	Backgrounds Good health Good citizen Other countries			
United States	Skills training Desire training	Skills – job Good health Good citizen	Other countries Backgrounds Self-confidence			

Note: The figures are for the combined "very" and "fairly" confident categories. "Skills and knowledge which will help in continuing studies or training" was not asked in the United Kingdom; this "quality" was added after the United Kingdom survey had begun.
Source: OECD, INES project.

Confidence in schools is highest in relation to further training. "Desire to continue studies or training" appears in Block 1 in seven countries, and "Skills and knowledge which will help in continuing studies or training" are in Block 1 in eight countries. On no other qualities is there such a unanimity of views. In terms of importance, "Understanding of other countries of the world" is in the lowest block for ten out of the twelve countries. When it comes to confidence, however, it tends to be noted more highly. In France, for example, it is in the lowest importance block but it is in the second highest confidence block. By contrast, the quality rated most highly in importance – "Self-confidence" – often receives a low confidence rating. In Finland, "Self-confidence" is in the highest importance block but it is rated in the lowest confidence block.

Breakouts

It is possible to examine this pattern in more details by using information from breakouts. Looking at self-confidence and comparing importance and confidence by age-group shows up some clear differences. Younger people are *more* likely than older people to see self-confidence as an essential priority for schools but have *less* confidence that it is developed well by schools, as is seen in Figure 6.7.

Similarly, it is possible to look at the differences between the views of males and females, parents and non-parents, and of variation by length of formal education. Women are more likely to view self-confidence as important but there is no difference between men and women in terms of confidence. Parents are more likely than non-parents to view it as essential and to be confident that it is being developed well (see Figure 6.8). Most marked of all are the differences between early school leavers and later leavers. The later leavers tend to feel more strongly that the quality is important but they are less confident that it is being developed well.

Summary

- Qualities are viewed as being as important as subjects.
- There is less confidence in important *Qualities* being well developed than in important subjects being well taught.
- Self-confidence" is consistently viewed as important in all countries.
- A "Desire to continue studies or training" and "Skills and knowledge which will help in continuing studies or training" are thought to be developed well in most countries.

4. Priorities for Schools in Achieving their Goals

The general public were also asked to give their views on what schools ought to emphasise in order to achieve their goals (see Figure 6.9).

Figure/*Graphique* 6.7. **Importance and confidence in the development of self-confidence by age-groups**
Importance du renforcement de la confiance en soi par groupe d'âge et degré d'optimisme dans ce domaine

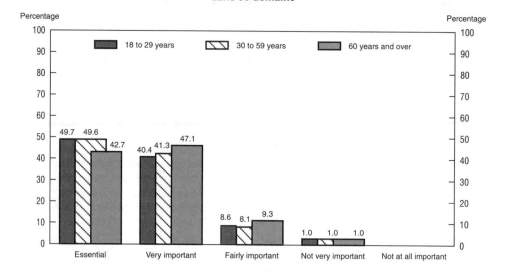

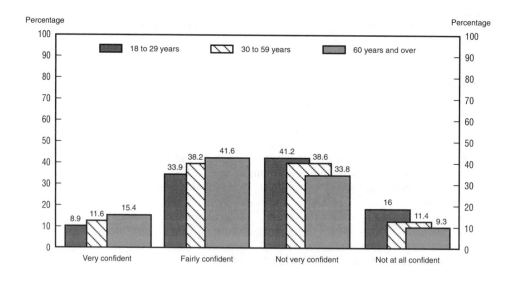

Source: OECD, INES project.

Figure/*Graphique* 6.8. **Importance and confidence in the development of self-confidence by parents/non-parents**
Importance accordée respectivement par les parents et non-parents au renforcement de la confiance en soi et degré d'optimisme dans ce domaine

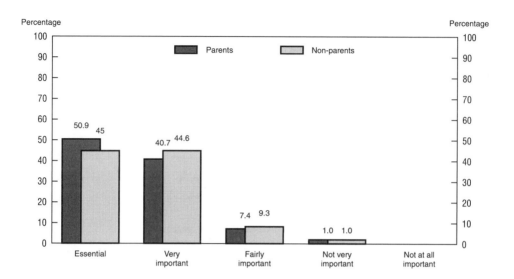

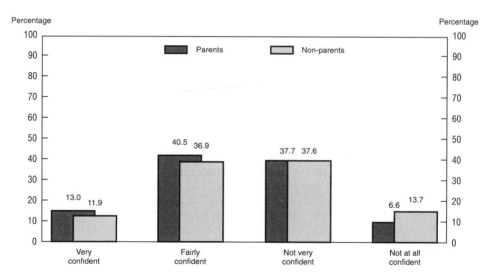

Note: Older people, non-parents, the early leavers group and women are consistently *more* likely to respond that they are "not sure".
Source: OECD, INES project.

83

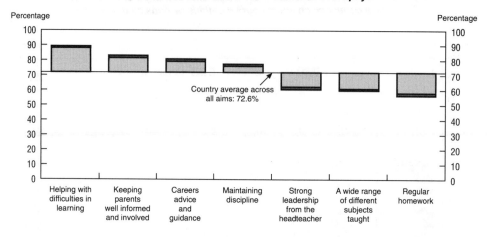

Figure/*Graphique* 6.9. **The importance of areas to emphasise using combined countries data**
*Importance des domaines sur lesquels il convient de mettre l'accent,
d'après les données relatives à l'ensemble des pays*

Note: The figures are for the combined "essential" and "very important" responses.
Source: OECD, INES project.

"Helping with difficulties in learning" emerges significantly as the highest priority across countries and is consistently rated in first place except in Finland and the United States. In both these countries, it is placed in the second highest block. In the bottom block is "Homework", then in the next block up availability of a "Wide range of subjects". These are not, however, ranked uniformly low by all countries. In Austria, "Homework" is ranked significantly higher than "Leadership of the head-teacher", but in France it is the other way around. Part of the variation between countries is shown in Table 6.5. This takes the seven priority areas and shows for each one the number of countries which gave it a relatively high or low marking. It illustrates the high level of agreement about some areas, and the wide disparity of views in others. For example, in ten countries, "Helping with difficulties in learning" is marked in the first priority block. "Discipline" and "Homework", by contrast, fall into five different blocks.

Breakouts

Figure 6.10 shows the percentage, across the seven areas, for parents and non-parents who replied "Essential" or "Very important". In all cases, apart from "Careers advice and guidance", the parents' responses are significantly different from those of the non-parents.

Table/Tableau 6.5.

Blocking by areas of emphasis

Fonctions jugées essentielles par les différents groupes

	Block 1	Block 2	Block 3	Block 4	Block 5	Block 6	Block 7
Careers advice and guidance	✕✕✕	✕✕✕	✕✕✕✕ ✕	✕			
Helping with difficulties in learning	✕✕✕✕ ✕✕✕✕ ✕✕	✕✕					
Strong leadership from the headteacher			✕✕✕✕	✕✕✕✕ ✕		✕✕✕	
Maintaining discipline	✕	✕✕✕✕ ✕✕	✕✕✕	✕	✕		
Regular homework			✕✕	✕✕✕✕	✕✕	✕✕	✕✕
A wide range of different subjects taught			✕✕	✕✕✕✕ ✕✕	✕✕✕✕		
Keeping parents well informed and involved	✕✕✕	✕✕✕✕ ✕✕	✕✕	✕			

Note: The figures are for the combined "essential" and "very important" responses.
Source: OECD, INES project.

There was less consistency in the views between age-groups. Older people were more likely than younger ones to respond with "Essential" to "Strong leadership", "Maintenance of discipline" and "Regular homework". This pattern emerges even more strongly between early and late leavers. Figure 6.11 shows areas in which there is a significant difference between the two groups. These are arranged from left to right in order of significance. The most significant difference is in relation to "Strong leadership", followed by "Maintaining discipline", then "Regular homework". On the last two items, "Range of subjects" and "Difficulties in learning", there is no difference between the two groups.

Individual Countries

An example of different patterns of response in individual countries is shown in Figure 6.12, which compares Austria and the United States on "Strong leadership" of headteachers. The pattern in Austria is typical in that the difference is significant and quite large. In the United States there is no difference between the response patterns of the two groups.

85

Figure/*Graphique* 6.10. **Views of parents and non-parents**
on the importance of areas to emphasise
Avis des parents et non-parents quant à l'importance des domaines
sur lesquels il convient de mettre l'accent

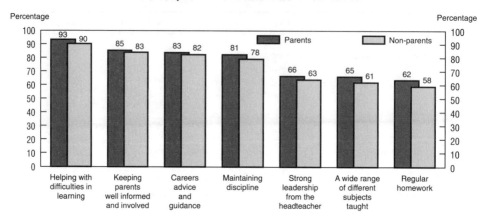

Note: The figures are for the combined "essential" and "very important" responses.
Source: OECD, INES project.

Figure/*Graphique* 6.11. **Views of the early and late leavers on the importance of areas to emphasise**
Avis des élèves ayant quitté l'école à un stade précoce ou tardif quant à l'importance
des domaines sur lesquels il convient de mettre l'accent

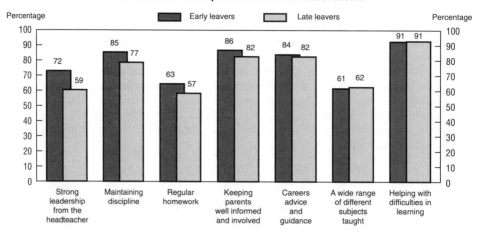

Note: The figures are for the combined "essential" and "very important" responses.
Source: OECD, INES project.

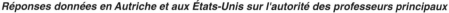

Figure/*Graphique* 6.12. **Responses in Austria and the United States on strong leadership of headteachers**
Réponses données en Autriche et aux États-Unis sur l'autorité des professeurs principaux

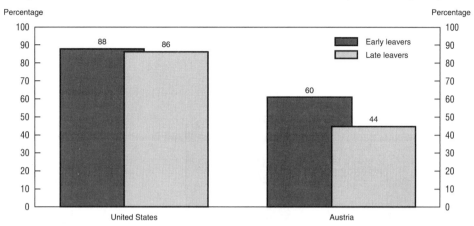

Source: OECD, INES project.

Figure 6.13 compares the Netherlands and Sweden for the item "Helping with difficulties in learning". It shows only responses for the three categories "Essential", "Very important" and "Fairly important" because less than 1 per cent replied "Not at all" or "Not very important". The Netherlands and Sweden are at opposite ends of a scale. The Netherlands is, of the seven countries in which the views of males and females are very similar, the country where the differences are least. Sweden is the country where the differences are most marked.

Summary

- Discrimination between each of the priority areas is strong in most countries.
- Helping with difficulties in learning is consistently viewed as important.
- Parents generally hold stronger views on the importance of each area than non-parents.
- There are considerable differences between the views of the different age-groups and between early and late leavers.

Figure/*Graphique* 6.13. **Responses in the Netherlands and Sweden on helping with difficulties in learning**
Réponses données aux Pays-Bas et en Suède sur l'aide à apporter aux élèves ayant des difficultés scolaires

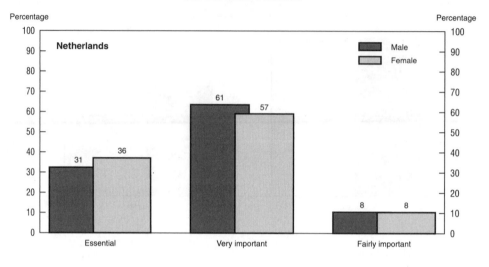

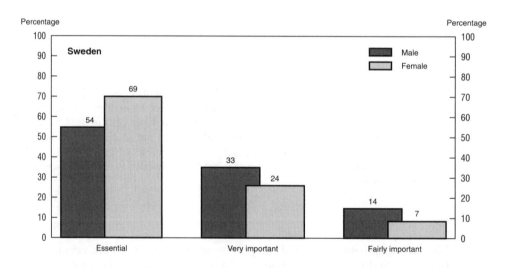

Note: The figures are for the combined "essential" and "very important" responses. Older people, non-parents, and early leavers are consistently *more* likely to respond that they are "not sure".
Source: OECD, INES project.

5. Personal and Social Development – Whose Responsibility?

The survey included a question designed to gauge the extent to which personal and social development was seen as a responsibility of home or school. While it might have been surprising if it were not generally seen as a shared responsibility, the degree of responsibility ascribed to the school did, in fact, differ from country to country, as is seen in Table 6.6.

How do these data relate to data on the development of qualities by schools and the areas the public feel schools should emphasise? The evidence suggests a slight association between responses to the question on the responsibility for the personal and social development of young people and to questions on importance of qualities. The link is strongest in relation to "Being a good citizen" and "Careers advice and guidance". In general, it appeared that the greater the responsibility of the home for personal and social

Table/Tableau 6.6.

Views on the responsibility for the personal and social development of young people by country

Points de vue exprimés par les différents pays quant à la responsabilité du développement personnel et social des jeunes

	Home should have more responsibility than school		Responsibility shared equally between home and school		Home should have less responsibility than school	
	%	S.E.	%	S.E.	%	S.E.
Denmark	55	1.5	43	1.5	2	0.4
Finland	55	1.4	44	1.4	1	0.3
Netherlands	44	1.6	53	1.6	3	0.5
Austria	42	1.2	55	1.2	3	0.4
Sweden	38	1.5	60	1.6	2	0.4
United States	34	1.3	63	1.4	3	0.5
Belgium (Flemish Community)	28	1.6	65	1.7	7	0.9
Portugal	18	1.1	67	1.3	14	1.0
Spain	15	1.0	80	1.1	5	0.6
United Kingdom	14	1.0	81	1.1	5	0.6
France	14	0.9	79	1.1	7	0.7
Combined countries	32.7	0.4	62.6	0.4	4.7	0.2

Note: The data from Switzerland on this question are not comparable to those of the other countries.
S.E. = Standard error.
Source: OECD, INES project.

Figure/*Graphique* 6.14. **Link between responsibility and "being a good citizen" and "careers advice and guidance"**
Lien entre la responsabilité et le « fait d'être un bon citoyen »
et « l'orientation professionnelle »

Percentage who think it is important for schools
to develop being a good citizen

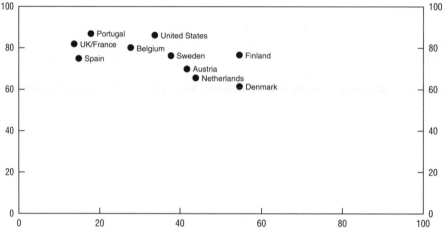

Percentage who think the home should have more responsibility than the school

Percentage who think schools should emphasise
careers advice and guidance

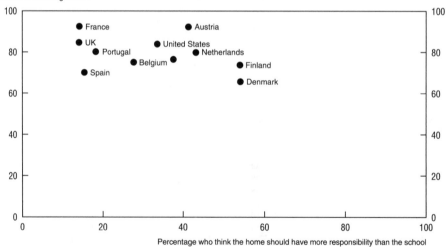

Percentage who think the home should have more responsibility than the school

Note: The figures for the importance on the vertical axis combine "essential" and "very important" responses. "Belgium" refers to the Flemish Community.
Source: OECD, INES project.

development, the lower the importance rating for "Being a good citizen" and "Careers advice and guidance". This relationship is illustrated in Figure 6.14.

Breakouts

There are significant variations for age, gender and length of formal education although not for parents as against non-parents. Both the older age group and the early leavers group are less likely to see the home as having more responsibility than the school. Non-parents are less likely to view the responsibility as shared equally between the home and school. The opposite holds true for women, who are more likely to see that responsibility as being shared.

Individual Countries

The significance of early or later school leaving varies between countries. It is significant in eight of the countries, with the difference being greatest in France. Figure 6.15 shows that 8 per cent of the early leavers group felt that the home should have more responsibility than the school compared to 17 per cent of late leavers.

Figure/*Graphique* 6.15. **Views in France on the balance of home/school responsibility for the personal and social development of young people by education group**
Avis exprimés en France sur le degré respectif de responsabilité des parents et de l'école dans le développement personnel et social des jeunes, selon le niveau d'instruction

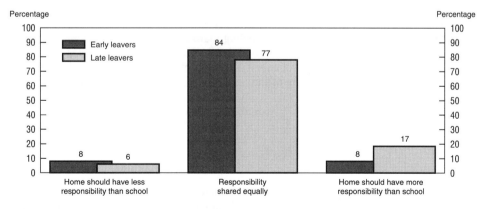

Note: Older people, non-parents, early leavers and women are consistently *more* likely to respond that they are "not sure".
Source: OECD, INES project.

Summary

- In all countries, except Denmark and Finland, the majority of the public think that the responsibility for personal and social education should be shared equally between home and school.
- The degree of emphasis on the home's responsibility for personal and social education is related to perceptions of the school's role in developing qualities such as citizenship.
- There is no difference between the views of parents and non-parents on the relative importance of the home and the school in the personal and social development of young people.

6. Locus of Decision-Making

The devolution of decision-making to schools is a policy issue. What the public perceive as important in school level decision-making provides a complement to existing INES indicators. The questionnaire suggested six possible areas of school level decision-making and offered five categories of reply from "Very important" to "Not at all important". Table 6.7 shows responses for each country, with "Very important" and "Fairly important" combined.

Table 6.7 shows that the majority of the public support greater school autonomy in all areas. Support is least consistent for decisions on "Teachers' salaries" and "Working conditions". In Denmark, Sweden and Switzerland, such decisions find support from less than half the population. France and the Netherlands are the exception in ranking "What subjects are taught" even lower. The table also shows that the public make some quite clear distinctions between what they see as most and least appropriate for school decision-making. There is a relatively strong feeling that schools should "Appoint their own staff". There is a less strong feeling that they should decide on their "Salaries". There is greater enthusiasm for school control over "Teaching methods" than over "Content" or "Time spent" per subject. Spending of the "Budget" is also generally rated as more of a school decision.

Breakouts

Women are more likely than men, in all the areas, to view it as more important for the school to take decisions. The difference is slight, although still significant, for the items on the "Budget" and on "Teacher selection and promotion". Early leavers are also more likely to be in favour of school level decision-making in all areas except for budget. Parents are more likely to believe that it is important for schools to decide on

Table/Tableau 6.7.

The percentage of respondents who felt is was "very important" or "fairly important" that the following decisions should be made by the school

Pourcentage de répondants estimant qu'il est «très important» ou «assez important» que les décisions suivantes soient prises par l'école

	How subjects are taught		How the school budget is spent		Teacher selection and promotion		Amount of time spent teaching each subject		What subjects are taught		Teachers' salaries and working conditions		Average over decision areas
	%	S.E.	%	S.E.	%	S.E.	%	S.E.	%	S.E.	%	S.E.	%
Austria	78	1.0	71	1.1	64	1.1	71	1.1	68	1.1	54	1.2	67.7
Belgium (Flemish Com.)	84	1.3	80	1.4	78	1.5	74	1.6	67	1.7	61	1.7	74.0
Denmark	80	1.2	78	1.2	78	1.2	54	1.5	56	1.5	40	1.5	64.3
Finland	86	1.0	85	1.0	79	1.2	80	1.2	68	1.4	65	1.4	77.2
France	90	0.8	86	0.9	87	0.9	89	0.8	76	1.1	79	1.0	84.5
Netherlands	81	1.3	79	1.3	88	1.1	68	1.5	52	1.6	58	1.6	71.0
Portugal	71	1.3	70	1.3	65	1.3	68	1.3	64	1.4	53	1.4	65.2
Spain	65	1.3	62	1.3	63	1.3	64	1.3	56	1.3	54	1.3	60.7
Sweden	83	1.2	85	1.1	81	1.2	69	1.5	58	1.6	45	1.6	70.2
Switzerland	76	1.4	62	1.6	65	1.5	65	1.5	57	1.6	45	1.6	61.7
United Kingdom	87	1.0	88	0.9	86	1.0	87	1.0	79	1.2	73	1.3	83.3
United States	86	1.0	87	1.0	88	0.9	85	1.0	81	1.1	83	1.0	85.0
Combined countries	80.6	0.3	77.8	0.3	76.8	0.4	72.8	0.4	65.2	0.4	59.2	0.4	

Source: OECD, INES project.

93

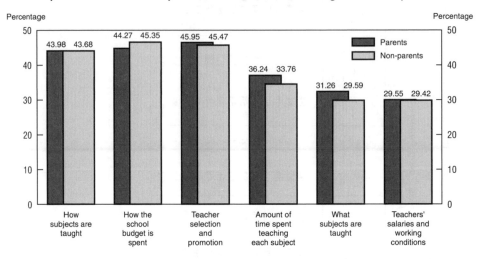

Figure/*Graphique* 6.16. **Importance of decisions at school level: "very important" category**
Importance des décisions prises au niveau de l'école : catégorie « très important »

Source: OECD, INES project.

"How much time is spent on each subject". They are also more likely to think it is "Fairly (as opposed to "not at all") important" for schools to decide on "Teachers' salaries and working conditions" (see Figure 6.16).

Individual Countries

There is considerable variation in these patterns among individual countries, which is illustrated by the example "Time spent teaching each subject". Table 6.8 shows country by country the percentage who responded "Very" or "Fairly important" from each of the two groups – early and later leavers. It also shows whether these differences are statistically significant.

Summary

- There is generally greatest support for schools' deciding on how subjects are taught and least support for schools' deciding on teachers' salaries and working conditions.
- Older people, early leavers and females are generally more inclined to think it is important for schools to take decisions.

Table/Tableau 6.8.

Education level responses by country on the importance of schools taking decisions on the amount of time spent teaching each subject

Importance attachée selon le degré d'instruction dans les différents pays à la prise par les écoles des décisions relatives au temps respectif consacré à l'enseignement des différentes matières

	Very and fairly important		Not very and not at all important		Comment
	Early leavers (%)	Late leavers (%)	Early leavers (%)	Late leavers (%)	
Austria	76	75	24	25	Not significant
Belgium (Flemish Community)	80	74	20	26	Not significant
Denmark	64	59	36	41	Not significant
Finland	82	79	18	21	Not significant
France	93	90	7	10	Significant
Netherlands	81	64	19	36	Significant
Portugal	89	92	11	8	Not significant
Spain	86	81	14	19	Significant
Sweden	84	69	16	31	Significant
United Kingdom	97	88	3	12	Significant
United States	93	89	7	11	Significant
Overall	84	77	16	22	Significant

Note: Older people, non-parents, early leavers and women are consistently *more* likely to respond that they are "not sure".
Source: OECD, INES project.

- Parents are, in some areas, more inclined than non-parents to view it as important that schools should take decisions. This is particularly true for how much time is spent teaching subjects and on teachers' salaries and working conditions.

7. Respect for Secondary-School Teachers

The perceived status of teachers and respect for the profession is an issue that is of concern not only to teachers but to a number of other constituencies and public agencies. The perceptions of the general public in different countries are, therefore, worth close scrutiny. In response to the question "How respected are secondary teachers as a profession?" there were very clear differences from country to country. Respondents were asked what they thought about the general level of respect for secondary teachers. There were five categories of response: "Very respected", "Fairly respected", "Not very respected", "Not at all respected" and "Not sure either way". Older people, non-parents, early leavers and women were consistently *more* likely to respond that they were "Not sure".

Breakouts

Table 6.9 summarises patterns of response for each of the breakout variables. Differences between age-groups, between early and late leavers, and between parents and non-parents are statistically significant. Differences between men and women are not.

Individual Countries

There are two countries where the association between gender and respect is significant: Portugal and the United Kingdom. In each case women tend to believe that the level of respect for teachers is higher. This gender difference is most significant in the United Kingdom where it is greater among non-parents than among parents (see Figure 6.17).

Although the differences between parental and non-parental responses is barely significant overall, Denmark is an exception. Danish parents are more likely than non-parents to say that teachers are respected. When gender is considered as a factor, together with parent/non-parent breakout, a further level of detailed information is revealed, as in Figure 6.18. It shows that male parents have a higher level of respect for teachers than

Table/Tableau 6.9.

Respect for teachers by breakout groups

(%)

Respect qu'inspirent les enseignants aux différents groupes

	Very or fairly respected	Not very or not at all respected	Comment
Parents	63 (0.73)	37 (0.73)	Significant difference between
Non-parents	61 (0.55)	39 (0.55)	parents and non-parents
First education-level group	65 (0.69)	35 (0.57)	Very highly significant difference
Second education-level group	59 (0.57)	41 (0.57)	between the education-level groups
Men	61 (0.63)	39 (0.63)	No significant difference
Women	62 (0.61)	38 (0.61)	between males and females
Up to 29 years	56 (0.86)	44 (0.86)	Very highly significant difference
30 to 59 years	62 (0.66)	38 (0.66)	between the age-groups
60 years and over	65 (0.67)	35 (0.67)	

Note: Standard errors are given in brackets. The data from Switzerland on this question are not comparable to those of the other countries.

Source: OECD, INES project.

Percentage

Figure/*Graphique* 6.17. **Level of respect by gender in the United Kingdom**
Degré de respect qu'inspirent les enseignants selon le sexe au Royaume-Uni

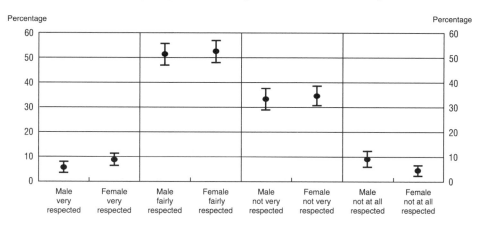

Note: A vertical line is drawn for males and for females for each level of respect. The percentage in the sample is the middle horizontal line. The percentage in the population lies somewhere between the top and bottom of the vertical line (the length of the vertical line reflects the confidence interval associated with the figures).
Source: OECD, INES project.

Figure/*Graphique* 6.18. **Level of respect by parental status among men in Denmark**
Degré de respect qu'inspirent les enseignants aux hommes, selon qu'ils sont parents d'élèves ou non au Danemark

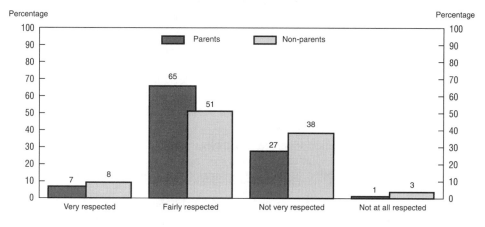

Note: Older people, non-parents, early leavers and women are consistently *more* likely to respond that they are "not sure".
Source: OECD, INES project.

men who are not parents, a difference that does not hold true for female parents compared with women who are not parents.

The age difference in level of respect for teachers is generally significant, but there are three countries – Portugal, Spain and the United States – where this is not true. Similarly, whilst the difference in the views of the early and late leavers is usually significant, there are three countries – Austria, Denmark and Spain – which do not follow the general pattern.

Summary

- Older people, early leavers and parents expressed a higher level of respect for teachers.
- A majority of the public in every country except Spain, think that teachers are very or fairly respected.

8.   Teachers' Salaries

The question "Should teachers earn more or less than they do now?" is, therefore, an interesting one which some countries decided to include in the questionnaire. The countries which did ask this question found that many respondents were not sure about how much teachers should be paid. Overall the "Not sure" category had a 24 per cent response, a very much higher "Not sure" figure than for other questions. Portugal and Spain had a particularly high "Not sure" response – nearly half of all respondents in Portugal and over a third in Spain. Figure 6.19 shows the response patterns in the nine countries which asked this question. For the sake of simplicity, the "Much more" and "A little more" categories have been combined, as have the "Much less" and a "Little less" responses. Only in the United States was the "Much more" category used to any considerable extent.

If the "Not sure" information is excluded, there is a clear majority of the public in the Netherlands (63 per cent), Portugal (63 per cent), and the United States (70 per cent) who think that teachers should be paid more, and in Belgium (Flemish Community) there is a slight majority (52 per cent).

There is some information to suggest that there may be a relationship between the public's views on teachers' salaries, their views on respect for teachers, and the salaries actually paid. If the information on teachers' salaries (from Network C) is mapped on to data about the perceived status of teachers, two countries stand out because they fall outside the general range, as is seen in Figure 6.20. In each of these, there is a clear relationship between level of pay and perceived status. In Spain, both status and views on pay are low and, in Austria, status is high but there is not a strong view that teachers should earn more. This picture is filled out a little when this information is placed alongside data on maximum salaries for secondary-school teachers.

Figure/*Graphique* 6.19. **Responses by country on teachers' salaries**
Réponses par pays sur les salaires des enseignants

Austria

Belgium (Flemish Community)

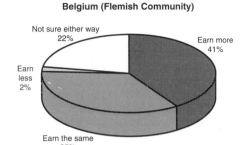

Denmark

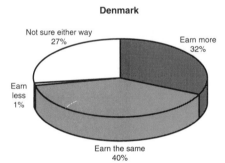

France

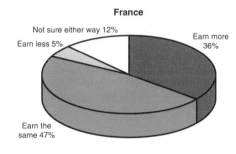

Netherlands

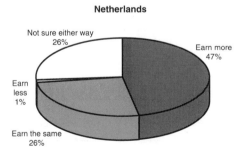

Portugal

Source: OECD, INES project.

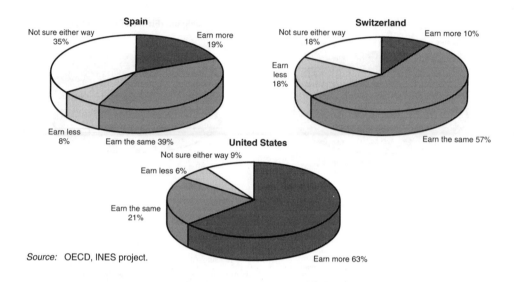

Figure/*Graphique* 6.19. **Responses by country on teachers' salaries** *(cont'd)*
Réponses par pays sur les salaires des enseignants (suite)

Source: OECD, INES project.

Table 6.10 shows the maximum salary of secondary-school teachers at purchasing power parities (PPP) rates. While nine countries asked the public about ''appropriate'' level of pay for teachers, only six are shown in the table. These are the six for which data on current salary as a PPP rate are available.

For the two outlying countries in Figure 6.20 (Austria and Spain), the information on teachers' salaries points to public satisfaction. In Austria, there is high respect for teachers, high relative pay and a belief that teachers' salaries are about right. In Spain, there is low respect for teachers, low pay and a belief that the pay is about right.

Breakouts

Fewer of the older age-group and early school leavers thought that teachers should earn more. This same pattern is seen among parents and women. The difference between early and late leavers can be seen most clearly in Portugal. Figure 6.21 shows the responses for the two groups. The percentage of early leavers who thought teachers should be paid more was about half that of late leavers, and the ''Not sure'' response is, in percentage terms, correspondingly higher among early leavers.

Figure/*Graphique* 6.20. **Percentage of respondents who think that teachers are "very"
or "fairly respected" by percentage who think they should be paid "much more"
or "a little more"**
*Pourcentage de répondants estimant que les enseignants sont « très respectés »
ou « assez respectés » rapporté au pourcentage de ceux qui estiment
qu'ils devraient être payés « beaucoup plus » ou « un peu plus »*

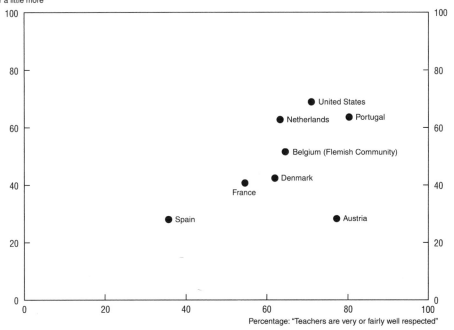

Percentage: "Teachers should be paid much more
or a little more"

Percentage: "Teachers are very or fairly well respected"

Note: "Not sure" responses have been excluded from the base of the calculation. Data on the level of respect for
teachers in Switzerland are not comparable to those for the other countries. The question on teachers' salaries
was not asked in the United Kingdom.
Source: OECD, INES project.

Summary

- The percentage of "unsure" responses was much higher in this question than in
the others.
- In some countries there was a strong view that teachers should be paid more; a
very low percentage thought that they should be paid less.
- Respect for teachers and views on pay followed a similar pattern in most of the
countries.

101

Table/Tableau 6.10.

Maximum salaries for secondary-school teachers in PPP rates

Salaires maximums des enseignants du secondaire en taux PPA

	Maximum pay	Percentage who think teachers should earn more
Austria	42 448	29
United States	37 146	70
Portugal	36 078	63
Netherlands	33 454	62
Belgium (Flemish Community)	31 308	52
Spain	30 632	27

Note: "Not sure" responses have been excluded from the base of the calculation.
Source: OECD, INES project.

Figure/*Graphique* 6.21. **Views on pay by early and late leavers in Portugal**
Avis sur la rémunération des enseignants des personnes ayant quitté l'école à un stade précoce ou tardif au Portugal

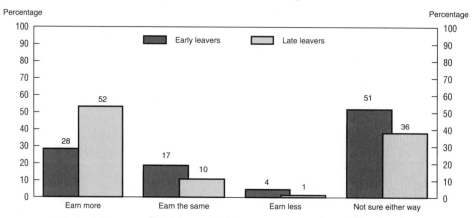

Note: Older people, non-parents, early leavers and women are consistently *more* likely to respond that they are "not sure".
Source: OECD, INES project.

9. What do the Figures Mean?

This chapter has presented the key findings from responses of the general public to the items included in the common survey. It has highlighted some of the central similarities and differences and indicated where figures should, and should not, be treated as statistically significant. The meaning or advanced hypotheses about what these figures might mean are studied in the next chapter.

Interpreting the Findings
Interprétation des résultats

by

John MacBeath
University of Strathclyde, Scotland

and

Carol Calvert
Scottish Office Education Department, Edinburgh, Scotland

What do all of the data mean, and what confidence can we have that it is telling us the truth? This chapter selects some of the key findings and considers what they might and might not mean in both national and international contexts. It is focused on areas where disaggregation may be helpful and unhelpful. It discusses the degree of caution that needs to be exercised in seeing the findings as definitive evidence or as indicators of something illuminating and of potential significance. Different ways of analysing attitudinal data are suggested, particularly in different cultural and linguistic contexts, where language and meaning are confounding variables.

*

*   *

Note de synthèse

Ce chapitre examine le sens des faits décrits au chapitre 6 d'une façon générale en posant des questions plutôt qu'en y répondant, en tentant de replacer dans leur contexte

105

les questions de politique générale, de culture et de langage et en renvoyant le cas échéant le lecteur à d'autres sources de données.

Il analyse ce que révèlent les données et les types d'investigations qui pourraient être entreprises pour trouver des explications. Bien que l'on puisse interpréter les statistiques telles quelles en comparant des pourcentages « bruts » entre pays, il conviendra surtout d'examiner la relativité des jugements en comparant les classements relatifs dans un même pays. Il ne faut pas perdre de vue le fait que dans le cadre des enquêtes de ce type, en particulier celles qui portent sur plusieurs pays, les normes et la qualité escomptées varient en fonction de l'évolution du climat politique et économique. Les décideurs peuvent, à un certain moment, avoir intérêt à susciter les plus grandes espérances, à encourager les gens à exiger davantage de services et à être plus critiques. Ce sont là autant de signaux qui doivent inciter les lecteurs à interpréter les données en faisant preuve d'esprit critique et de prudence.

Néanmoins, il existe également un certain nombre de messages dépourvus de toute ambiguïté à l'intention des décideurs au sujet du rôle de l'école et des buts de l'enseignement. Cette observation vaut particulièrement sur deux points : les priorités et objectifs clés et le fait que le public compte moins sur l'école pour développer des qualités importantes que pour enseigner des matières importantes. « La confiance en soi » constitue un exemple frappant de ce phénomène. Quelles que soient les autres conclusions pouvant être tirées de cet « indicateur de lacunes », les éléments d'information disponibles laissent à penser que l'école doit faire davantage pour convaincre le public que la confiance en soi peut avoir un rang de priorité élevé.

Les informations sur l'épanouissement personnel, le développement social et l'instruction civique fournissent également des messages quant à la politique à suivre. Dans un certain nombre de pays, les responsables politiques et les sociologues sont, depuis quelques années, de plus en plus préoccupés par le déclin de la cellule familiale, par l'aggravation de la délinquance juvénile et par la diminution apparente du sens des responsabilités et de la discipline parentale. Dans beaucoup de pays de l'OCDE, on s'efforce à la fois de renforcer le sens des responsabilités au sein du foyer et de faire en sorte que l'école contribue davantage à la formation personnelle et sociale (ainsi qu'à l'instruction civique). Ce phénomène s'accompagne dans beaucoup de pays de tentatives visant à établir des liens plus solides entre la famille et l'école. Si, d'un point de vue de politique générale, on veut renforcer l'esprit civique, il faudra prendre en compte la façon dont différents groupes envisagent les rapports entre l'école et la famille ainsi qu'entre enseignants et parents. Un indicateur dans ce domaine peut servir à la longue de baromètre du changement social et de l'évolution des attitudes du public.

L'importance considérable constamment accordée à « l'aide à apporter aux élèves qui ont des difficultés scolaires » a également des incidences quant à la politique à suivre, parce que cette préoccupation est la plus proche de la mission de l'école et reflète les conclusions des recherches effectuées sur l'idée que se font les parents et les élèves d'un enseignement efficace. Cet objectif ainsi que d'autres objectifs hautement prioritaires sont d'actualité dans les pays qui ont décidé d'élever d'ici l'an 2000 le niveau des connaissances de l'ensemble de la population.

Les différences entre les pays quant à l'importance relative accordée à l'autorité, à la discipline et aux devoirs à la maison débouchent sur un débat intéressant sur les différences linguistiques et culturelles ainsi que sur les différences de priorité quant à la politique à suivre. Deux domaines prioritaires classés de façon très différente sont « les devoirs à la maison » (faible degré de priorité) et « la participation des parents » (degré de priorité élevé). Si les devoirs à la maison sont aussi importants que l'indiquent les recherches, la politique ou les pratiques suivies peuvent avoir des lacunes qui méritent d'être étudiées de façon plus approfondie.

Ce que le public a à dire sur la responsabilité de l'école dans la prise de décision constitue un ensemble d'informations importantes sur la politique à suivre, d'autant plus que l'on constate certaines opinions résolues et des préférences très marquées. Il faut manifestement prendre en compte la question de la base d'informations à partir de laquelle de tels jugements sont formulés, question qui relève elle-même de la politique générale. Le niveau de sensibilisation peut différer non seulement d'un pays à l'autre, mais aussi d'un groupe à l'autre dans un même pays. Ces disparités internes peuvent être l'indicateur le plus significatif pour un pays quel qu'il soit.

Le respect des enseignants constitue une autre question d'une importance considérable, mais c'est probablement dans ce domaine que l'ensemble des données est le plus difficile à interpréter. Les comparaisons entre groupes sont utiles, par exemple, en ce sens qu'elles font apparaître des différences au niveau de la durée de l'enseignement suivi par les répondants. Ce sont ceux qui ont fait les études les plus courtes qui ont le plus tendance à respecter les enseignants sans toutefois préconiser un relèvement de leurs traitements. C'est une constatation qui peut être approfondie et expliquée à l'aide d'autres données générales. Là encore, le contexte est utile pour expliquer pourquoi dans certains pays, on observe un rapport relativement constant entre le respect qu'inspirent les enseignants et leur niveau de rémunération, mais pas dans d'autres. C'est là un indicateur dont l'utilisation sera confirmée à la longue.

Toutes ces observations ne font que rappeler que l'interprétation nécessite une approche mesurée, plutôt qu'une approche consistant simplement à mesurer.

*

*   *

1.   The Tip of an Iceberg

The primary purpose of the questionnaires and the data which they generated was to support a set of indicators for inclusion in *Education at a Glance* (OECD, 1995). As has been seen in Chapter 6, however, the publication of seven indicators in *Education at a Glance* are only the tip of an iceberg whose bulk lies below the water line. What is on view, at a glance, is evidence of something deeper which invites further exploration.

2. The Search for Meaning

What then is revealed by the data, what lines of enquiry might be pursued, and what caveats have to be borne in mind when interpreting statistical indicators? The search for meaning has to look at the data in different ways:

- by taking the statistics at *face value*. That is, if 58 per cent of the Swiss public rate "Being a good citizen" as an "Essential" or "Very important" priority for the school curriculum, that is a positive result;
- by looking at *relativity* in judgements, for example, by comparing one country with other countries. By this measure, "Being a good citizen" is ranked low in Switzerland in comparison with the country average of 74.9 per cent;
- by comparing *relative ranking within one country*. "Being a good citizen" is ranked last among the eight Swiss priorities, across which there is a qualities average of 80.4 per cent.

These relative rankings do not invalidate the actual figures, but they are useful because they give weight to the notion of "importance". When designing the questionnaire, network members were conscious that the subjects of the enquiry would generally be seen positively ("of course learning native language is a good thing"), and they therefore saw the need for the questionnaire to be skewed to the positive end. So, by asking people to discriminate between "Essential", "Very important" and "Fairly important", a priority order emerged. It has to be borne in mind, then, when reading the figures, that the 58 per cent rating for "Being a good citizen", say, would become 85.2 per cent if those saying "Fairly important" were also included.

Statistically it would have been possible to weight country responses rather than report straight percentages. This would have facilitated a comparison of country rankings on the same scale and might have eliminated some of the bias that creeps in through language and culture. However, it would have been both difficult to read and interpret. How would a reader have been able to relate the statistics to what people were actually saying? It would have been misleading and would devalue what a respondent actually said when he or she responded "Very confident" or "Confident". In other words, such weighting would have built in another layer of researchers' assumptions which would have to be explained, and justified, to the reader.

In surveys of this kind, especially across countries, timing is a factor to be taken into account. Expectations of standards and quality will be different in different places and at different times because of the changing political and economic climate, or because of on-going school reform. It may be in policy-makers' interests at a certain point in time to raise expectations, to encourage people to demand more of the service and to be more critical. In Spain, for example, there is currently intense debate about educational reform, and if that were to raise their level of expectation it might commensurately lower their level of satisfaction, or their confidence in standards of delivery. All of these considerations should serve as signals to readers to approach the interpretation of indicators both critically and with caution, and wherever possible to examine the relativity of responses within a country. Indicators are not in themselves measures, but they do open the door to critical questions.

Policy analysts can help in interpreting the data for decision-makers by:

- cross-referencing wherever possible between attitude indicators [for example, how importantly do the Swiss rate citizenship *as a subject* (indicator C21 in the 1995 version of *Education at a Glance*), and how do they rate "Being a good citizen" as a school priority (indicator C22)?]
- checking against country policy (see Chapter 4 and the country statement in the network's technical report in Bosker, 1995);
- checking against other INES *Education at a Glance* indicators.

This chapter examines and considers the findings under broad headings related to the questions in the questionnaire (see Annex 2 to this volume), and raises policy issues.

3. The School Curriculum: Do the Responses Reflect National Goals?

Four of the items in the questionnaire (Questions 1-4) were about the curriculum, two about timetabled subjects and two about cross-curricular "qualities", including skills, attitudes and awareness. These subjects and qualities were included because they were common to all countries. This is in itself an interesting "finding" as it says something about the common purpose of schooling in countries which are culturally, economically and politically very different. The political will to fund such a question-naire may also be treated as "evidence". It suggests that the public at large have views and answers which are worth listening to.

Those answers, as expressed in the responses to Question 1, are sometimes fairly unequivocal and sometimes ambiguous. There are subjects which are seen in all countries as comprising a curricular core and others generally seen as of lesser importance. If the pattern of responses does not come as a surprise, it is because it reflects a widely accepted "common sense" view about the importance of mathematics, say, compared with that of the arts. That common sense is, to a degree, shaped by national policy and institutional-ised by school practice, but to *what* degree is the question to which policy-makers and opinion-makers would like an answer. Some parts of the public have been involved in the national debate about the mandatory school curriculum in a number of countries as a matter of policy, and changes have been made as a consequence of that public debate. In Sweden, for example, the proposal to reduce mandatory teaching hours in physical education was so strongly opposed by the public that they were restored to their previous status.

A move towards national goals and/or a national curriculum has been a common trend in many of the Member countries. The United States, for example, established National Education Goals in 1989, one of which was that by the year 2000 the United States would be first in the world in mathematics and science achievement. Mathematics is, as in other countries, ranked highly, but the relatively high ranking given to the sciences by the American public stands out from the order of priorities in other countries.

Mathematics appears to have secured a pre-eminent place in the curriculum, appar-ently without much challenge by policy-makers or public to that status. Evidence from the International Studies in Educational Achievement of the International Association for the Evaluation of Educational Achievement (IEA) reinforces both its perceived importance and its place in the curriculum. The second IEA mathematics study concluded that a majority of students wanted to do well in mathematics and saw it as important to future jobs. It adds: "They also indicate that their parents share these opinions and that their parents encourage and exhort them to do well in mathematics" (Postlethwaite and Wiley, 1992).

In Spain, curricular time for mathematics has actually been reduced within the last few years but it still figures at the top of the public's priority list. In the Netherlands, where mathematics is seen as important, it is nevertheless, ranked relatively low by comparison with other countries and by comparison with how the Dutch view foreign languages (69 per cent for mathematics as against 85 per cent for foreign languages). For policy-makers in that country it suggests that there may be a need to improve the status of mathematics in schools, while confirming at the same time that the status of foreign languages is already high in the public's eyes.

The significance of foreign languages in the Netherlands offers a further interesting contrast with the United States. Why should they be seen as so much less of a priority in the United States? When the data are taken together with those of the other English-speaking country in the survey, the United Kingdom, does it suggest that the perceived lower priority is due to political, economic and social place of English in world trade and tourism? By the same token, does the higher rating for foreign languages than for native languages in Finland reveal a perceived public desire to increase that country's influence internationally? In Spain too, foreign languages are rated marginally higher than the native language. Does this reflect a policy shift in 1990 which gave more curricular time to foreign languages and less to Castilian Spanish and mathematics? And is Austria's rating of foreign languages on a par with native language relevant to its forthcoming membership of the European Union?

The above questions are highly speculative and elusive, but the country reports do offer some illuminating insights. When the Swiss looked at differences among their three national language groups, they came up with a complex equation. Although native, or school language is rated more highly than foreign languages in the country as a whole, there are important differences within various language groups. German-speakers rate German well ahead in first place, followed by English, with French, another national language, well behind (83, 74, 63 per cent respectively). The French-speaking Swiss, on the other hand, rate English, French and German in that order (87, 83 and 74 per cent respectively) (Hutmacher and Gros, 1994).

In interpreting rankings of important and less important subjects we may also ask whether some subjects register more easily in the public mind because they are long-standing and seem intrinsic to the nature of schools. There could be a case for arguing that such subjects would be accorded higher priority than others of more recent vintage, such as information technology, for example. Yet, not only is information technology given a relatively high rating in all countries but sharp distinctions are drawn between it and technology (or technical studies), signalling both a public awareness of the difference and a clear discrimination between their relative degrees of importance.

It may, of course, be implicit within people's responses that their view of priorities is shaped by their opinion on whether subjects fall within, or outwith, the daily timetable. For example, mathematics is something to be done in school and would be seen as an unlikely spare time hobby, whereas the arts would flow across school boundaries and be pursued through school clubs, choirs and orchestras, exhibitions and festivals, or through individual leisure activities.

4. How are Distinctions Made among Desirable Qualities?

It might have been hypothesised that the general public would give lower priority to skills or aptitudes which have no established place within the curriculum. Yet the indicators derived from the answers to Question 3 show a high level of agreement across countries, not just about the importance of qualities in general but about specific qualities, such as self-confidence. Self-confidence may, in the public mind, be closely related to other highly rated qualities, such as skills for jobs and further training. All may be seen as contributing to young people's fitness for life and work and, it might be argued, mark the school's most important instrumental purpose.

The combined countries average for all but one of the qualities listed is 75 per cent or higher, with little differentiation between the highest and lowest-rated quality as well as among the eight qualities suggested. The quality ranked fairly consistently in the lowest priority block was "An understanding of other countries of the world". In every country it was rated below that country's own "Qualities average", and in France, Switzerland, the United Kingdom and the United States, it is at least ten percentage points behind the next highest quality. Why, in today's global village should "Understanding of other countries" be rated generally as a lower priority? It may be because it was the only one out of eight items in which the term "understanding" (an intellectual process) is used, while other items refer to skills and "how to". This may explain why the related item, "How to live among people from different backgrounds", fares considerably better, even in the four countries which gave a relatively low rating to "Understanding other countries".

How much can be inferred from these differences in ranking from country to country? How much do they say about what people in different countries want of their schools? Are they saying something equally important about social attitudes? Do they, for example, reveal something about the inward or outward perspectives of the public in different countries? Whatever is made of these statistics – and there is room for both too much and too little to be made of them – there is a need to be careful not to read into these relative rankings pessimistic messages. It has to be borne in mind that the actual or raw figures convey a generally optimistic message – that in virtually all cases a substantial majority of the public believe that all eight qualities constitute an "Essential" or "Very important" priority for schools.

Policy-makers in individual countries will still worry about the perceived values of some things relative to others. Danish and Dutch policy-makers may be concerned that good health and good citizenship are ranked very low in relative terms in their countries, given their importance as issues of social policy and national consequence.

Further light is thrown on this when these figures are compared with another indicator – "Responsibility for social and personal development of young people" (*cf.* Question 6). The public in France, Portugal, Spain and the United Kingdom ascribe considerably less responsibility to the home for personal and social development. For example, in Denmark and Finland, it is seen as the home's main responsibility by 55 per cent, compared with 18 per cent in Portugal and 14 per cent in the United Kingdom. A closer look at Portugal and the United Kingdom is illuminating. In the United Kingdom, "Education for citizenship" was rated as "Essential/Very important" as a subject by 36 per cent of the public, well below the subject average for that country. In Portugal it was rated as "Essential/Very important" by 73 per cent, well above the subject average. However, the quality "Being a good citizen", was rated "Essential/Very important" by 82 per cent in the United Kingdom (well above the United Kingdom average rating for qualities) and in Portugal by 87 per cent (above the average rating for qualities in that country). In other words, it appears that as a school priority, citizenship is not actually valued more in Portugal than in the United Kingdom but that it is institutionalised differently in schools in those two countries. In Portugal, it appears on the school timetable as an alternative to religious education, in every year of school; in the United Kingdom it rarely appears on a school timetable in that precise form but would be pursued through the school ethos as a whole or through programmes of personal and social education.

5. The Importance of Subjects and Qualities, and the Public's Confidence in the System

While there is a host of unanswered and intriguing questions, there are also some quite unequivocal messages for policy-makers about the role of schools and the purposes of teaching in the answers to Questions 2 and 4. There is a striking degree of uniformity among countries as to key subjects and priorities. Even more striking, perhaps, is lower confidence in schools' effectiveness with regard to the important qualities; in all countries this is lower than the importance accorded to subjects, with the exception of Portugal.

This comparison between importance and confidence is, among all indicators, perhaps the most generative of hypotheses, and it offers potentially the richest source of data for policy-makers. Their attention will immediately be drawn to the quality "Self-confidence". Its development is rated by the public in all countries as a priority for schools, yet the public's faith in schools' ability to develop it effectively is much more equivocal. Finland offers the most dramatic example of that. "Self-confidence" is placed in priority Block 1 in terms of importance, but in priority Block 5 (bottom) in terms of confidence. The same disparity, if sometimes less extreme, is evident in eight other countries.

How are the findings to be interpreted? Are they saying something about people's lack of certainty about where or how that quality is actually taught and learned, or are such judgements based on the evidence of the real live "products" which emerge from the system – the young people themselves? The fact that parents are, by comparison with non-parents, generally more positive may be seen as an optimistic finding given their closeness to the system. However, this has to be balanced against evidence from another group whose experience is, in some respects, even closer to the reality of schools, that is the 18-29 year age-group. They are markedly less positive than their elders about the success of schools in developing that quality.

Whatever else may be concluded from this *"gap" indicator* (the comparison between importance and confidence), the evidence suggests that schools in most of the countries represented here have to do more to convince the public at large that they too see "Self-confidence" as a priority and are improving their effectiveness in addressing it. This is perhaps the clearest and least equivocal message that may be taken from this data, but it raises other intriguing questions too. Where does that consistency of view about the importance of "Self-confidence" come from? Why is it so uniform across different countries and cultures? And what is the basis for that relative lack of confidence in schools with regard to their performance?

Researchers would like to pursue the questions: What are people using as their personal evidential base? For example, if parents use their children as their source of evidence of school quality, this may explain why non-parents were, in all countries, more likely than parents to use the "Not sure" category. This raises the further question: Are parents' views liable to be more informed, or less objective, than those of non-parents? Are there implications here for policy-makers as to how they might inform parents and the public at large about educational development and change?

How the "Not sure" category was used also differed from country to country. Also, is it significant that women are more likely to use the "Not sure" category than men? So, in any interpretation of the findings, account has to be taken of how prepared those different publics were to be dogmatic or cautious in offering their opinions, and of how much this varied by different social groups within and between countries. Are there national traits which underlie the way "Confidence" is expressed in different cultures?

The findings show, for example, that there is a difference between how "Essential" and "Very important" were used in different countries – but for what reason? There is, for example, a marked difference between Austria and Spain in the use of these catego-ries, which may say something about the willingness of respondents in those two coun-tries to make unequivocal statements. The nuances and weight of the term "Essential" in Austria and Spain (*Absolut nötig* and *Esencial,* respectively) are a factor to be taken into account. What culturally-shaped perceptions of the imperative lie behind the words? The fact that such differences exist, and may be underpinned by cultural and linguistic factors, re-emphasises the need to examine relativity of ranking *within* countries.

6. Responsibility for Personal and Social Development

The issue of "Personal and social development" (Question 6) was chosen for use as an indicator because it acts as a proxy for a significant set of policy issues, that is, the importance of home education, school education, and the inter-relationship of the two. Politicians and social commentators in a number of countries have been increasingly concerned in recent years about the decline of the nuclear family, the rise in juvenile crime, and a perceived diminishing of responsibility and parental discipline. There are in many OECD countries twin thrusts of policy demanding greater responsibility from the home and asking for personal and social education (and education for citizenship) to be built more strongly into the school ethos and curriculum. This is accompanied in many countries by attempts to forge stronger links between parents and teachers. The public's views on this are the subject of indicator C24. There is a need to ask what the responses to this indicator are saying.

The evidence points to some unambiguous conclusions as well as to some questions which are less readily answerable. It reveals that a solid proportion of the population in all countries sees this as a shared home-school priority (although in two countries the proportion is just less than half the population). It shows that more than one in three among the population in six countries view it as the main responsibility of the home, with very few people in any country seeing it as the main responsibility of the school.

The finding that men are more likely than women, in some countries, to see "Personal and social development" as a responsibility of the school may be an intriguing issue for further exploration. It may indeed prove to be significant in more than just the statistical sense.

The fact that there is, in most countries, a significant difference in people's views by length of formal education also raises interesting questions. There is (most notably in France, Sweden and the United States) more of a tendency for people who have stayed on in formal education to ascribe main responsibility to the home for personal and social education. Can it be inferred that the longer the exposure to formal education, the greater the confidence in the role of the parent as social educator? Does longer schooling bring with it a greater emphasis on the school's academic, as opposed to socialising, functions? Or is there no such cause and effect relationship? Evidence suggests that those who stayed longer at school were enabled to do so because of parental support (Walberg, 1985) and because of the "cultural capital" in the home (Bourdieu, 1977). The views of those "stayers" might, therefore, be saying something about their own experience of the home-school relationship.

However, it must be noted that there is a considerable degree of overlap in some countries between the early school leavers group and the older age-group. Among OECD countries, the minimum school leaving age has generally been rising progressively, as has the percentage of the population staying on at school. Given that older people are more likely to ascribe responsibility to the home, it would be reasonable to find the same tendency among the early leavers.

The lack of any significant difference by length of formal education in Austria, Denmark and Spain simply adds a further layer of complexity to the interpretation, giving us another question for further exploration. The answers to those further questions are worth finding because, while researchers may wish to go no further than stating, associations and correlations between factors, policy-makers and practitioners want to know about causes and effects. This is likely to be particularly true in relation to education in the home, parental involvement with the school, and the schools' role in education for citizenship.

Chapter 6 suggests that the degree to which people see ''Citizenship'' as an important school objective is related to the degree to which they see the school having, or sharing, a role in ''Personal and social education''. If then, from a policy point of view, ''Citizenship'' is to move up the policy agenda, it will benefit by taking into account just how different groups of people view the relationship between school and home, teachers and parents. It may be useful for policy-making purposes to develop an indicator over time which acts as a barometer of social change and of the corresponding attitudes of the public to national policy and school practice.

7. The Importance of School Practices

Into which areas of school practice would the general public like to see energies and resources being directed? So that we might gauge their expectations, people were asked in Question 5 to rate seven areas of priority in terms of their importance. As was the case with attitudes to subjects and qualities, all seven aspects tended to be seen as either ''Essential'' or ''Very important'' and we have to look for finer discriminations at the positive end in order to judge the relative weight of priorities. The areas covered were: careers advice and guidance, help with learning difficulties, strong leadership, maintaining discipline, regular homework, a wide range of different subjects taught, and keeping parents well informed and involved.

There is little room for ambiguity in the ranking ''Helping with difficulties in learning'', which was rated consistently highly across countries. Perhaps this is because, of all seven items, it is the one that comes closest to the essence of schooling, and echoes research findings into parents', and pupils', criteria for measuring the effectiveness of schools (Walberg, 1985; MVA Consultancy and MacBeath, 1989). The two other priorities ranked consistently highly are of a similar nature. They are both concerned with information and guidance – one about informing and involving parents, the other about informing and guiding pupils on future employment. But these priorities have also been the focus of policy initiatives as part of the moves to open up schools and to increase accountability, for example, in Denmark, the United Kingdom and the United States.

These three issues receive quite consistent support across countries, again perhaps because they are high-profile policy issues. All may be seen as contributing to a common policy to keep young people within the education system, to raise overall standards of achievement and to provide support for continued learning. By the year 2000, France aims to have 100 per cent of an age cohort receiving a minimum level of education qualification. It may, therefore, be reassuring to policy-makers to see ''Helping with dificulties in learning'' and ''Careers guidance'' at the top of the French public's agenda. ''Careers guidance'', at the head of Austria's list, reflects a national concern and policy debate over the drop-out rate, which has been accompanied in that country by a move to more intensive and effective forms of guidance, beginning in the lower secondary school.

On the four other items there is less consistency among countries. Maintaining discipline is highly rated by the general public in some, but not all, countries. In Austria, Denmark, Portugal and Spain, it is seen as relatively less important. What is it that accounts for such differences? The concept of "discipline" takes us into interesting cultural and linguistic territory. In Finland, the word may be translated by *kuri* (requiring obedience) or by *tyørauha* (work peace). Such linguistic subtleties are not just a feature of cross-country surveys of this kind, though, but are endemic to language itself. The term "discipline" is, like most educational vocabulary, socially constructed. In English, it carries a range of possible meanings from punishment and dominance to self-discipline, or a sense of order ("work peace"). However, we are given some clues to how terms such as discipline were interpreted by the public. Country reports are again a help. In Switzerland, responses were categorised by political affiliation – Left, Right, and no affiliation. This provided some significant differences, with "Maintaining discipline" being favoured much more by those on the political Right. The Right were also significantly more in favour of homework and strong leadership by the headteacher (Hutmacher and Gros, 1993).

Breakouts by age-group showed the older age consistently favouring discipline, homework and leadership, while the younger age group were more inclined to favour "Helping with difficulties in learning", "Careers advice" and "A wide range of subjects". Whether or not this may be read as a dichotomy between those favouring institutional control and those favouring greater pupil-centredness is open to debate, but factor analysis across the whole sample of countries does show these six items as falling into two distinctly different clusters (Bosker, 1995).

Views also differ according to length of formal education. When data from all countries are taken together, the two items which stand out prominently from the others are "Discipline" and "Strong leadership of the headteacher". While this may be taken as further evidence of the association between these two factors, it is interesting to find the early leavers as the group most likely to give to both a high priority rating. This same sharp contrast is found in some countries but not in others (this is graphically illustrated in the comparison between Austria and the United States – see Figure 6.12). The magnitude of these differences does raise questions. Are they, in fact, saying something about the relationship between educational and social structures in those countries? Is there a need to look a little more closely at the social make-up of those two groups in the relevant societies?

There is immediately a correlation between *older age-groups* and *early leaving,* more pronounced in some European countries than others and less a feature in the United States, which has traditionally retained a larger percentage of the population in upper secondary school than any European country. While this provides further correlation rather than further explanation, it does invite consideration of ways in which differential school experience may affect, and be affected by, attitudes and values in different countries.

Other factors also come into play, however. Attitudes to discipline and strong leadership are clearly not simply a matter of length of formal education, age and political affiliations. The data suggest that these attitudes are features of schools which are valued differently in different countries, reflecting both differences in culture and in policy and practice. In countries where "Leadership" is rated relatively highly (France, the United Kingdom and the United States), experience shows that schools can change dramatically with the coming or going of a headteacher. Research into leadership and school effects has consistently provided evidence of the importance of the head, or principal, as a feature of effective schools in the United States and the United Kingdom (Brookover, 1979; Mortimore *et al.*, 1988). By contrast, school effects in the Netherlands have not identified leadership as a factor in enhancing effectiveness (Scheerens, 1992). This is explained, in the Netherlands, by a tendency to view the headteacher as *primus inter pares*, or "first among equals". It is a view of leadership shared by the Danes, among whom there is a greater structural, as well as philosophical, emphasis on a team approach to school management than would be the case in France, the United Kingdom and the United States.

Nor is the headteacher factor a correlate of effectiveness in Spain. It is not surprising, therefore, that the public there also rate it as the lowest of their seven priorities. This may be interpreted in that country as an endorsement of a policy democratising schools by giving more power to teachers and to Schools Councils, which now elect the headteacher. The relatively low priority given to "Leadership" in the Netherlands and Spain should not, however, be allowed to obscure the fact that in both those countries this issue is viewed differently according to length of formal education, with early school leavers more inclined to emphasise it as a priority.

It is also interesting to consider differences in ranking accorded by the public to the remaining areas. The importance of keeping parents well informed is a growing policy issue in all country surveys, and this is reflected in the statistics. The lower priority given to it in some countries may be a hangover of a traditional belief that public institutions are there to provide public services and that it is the teachers' job to get on with it. The fact that "Keeping parents well informed" is at the top of the United States priority list may well reflect a long-standing tradition in that country of parental involvement in school-wide policy and day-to-day practice.

There is, among countries generally, less priority given to the item "A wide range of subjects taught". This probably cannot be taken to mean that public are against variety and choice, but is more likely to mean that they are generally satisfied with what is on offer or do not see it currently as a matter of particular concern. In three of the four countries where it is ranked in the lowest priority block (Denmark, Portugal and the United States), there has traditionally been a wide curriculum, although in all three countries there are current initiatives to tighten the focus and range of what is taught in lower secondary school. In Finland, only 29 per cent of the public saw "Range" as an important priority, perhaps reflecting satisfaction with the national curriculum, which has traditionally left little room for individual choice.

Homework is also given a relatively low priority, ranked in the lowest priority block by eight countries. In some cases that low ranking is corroborated by evidence from the IEA studies. For example, in those studies, Sweden was singled out for mention as the country in which pupils of secondary-school age spent the least amount of time on homework (Robitaille and Garden, 1989). Yet in Belgium (Flemish Community), where pupils reported more time on homework than virtually any other IEA country, the public were at one with the Swedes in ranking it seventh out of Network D's seven areas of priority. Caution has to be exercised, since the IEA studies were conducted in the early and mid-1980s, but for many of the general public that is, in fact, their reference point for making judgements about the value, and priority of, homework. Homework is, like discipline, a word with many resonances, and may be seen as anything from a dreary time-serving ritual to an integral part of learning. Recent research in a number of countries has emphasised the importance of recasting "homework" in terms of home learning and home support and raising its profile on the policy agenda (Cairney and Munsie, 1992; Merttens and Hannon, 1993; MacBeath and Turner, 1990). While that research has demonstrated how it is used in some schools as a mechanism for both informing and involving parents, the ranking of the two priorities in this survey – "Homework" (low) and "Parental involvement" (high) – suggests that such a connection is not being made by the public at large nor by the parent sub-group. This might point to a policy gap which deserves further scrutiny.

8.   The Importance of Decision-Making: Devolved Management by Schools

The questionnaire invited the public in Question 7 to give their views on "How important is it that the following decisions are made by the individual school itself?" The devolution of power to schools to take decisions for themselves is a trend to be observed in some form in all countries which took part in the survey. Moreover, enhanced powers of decision-making at school level are now widely accepted as desirable. Although all countries are moving in that direction, some exhibit more caution than others. In some previously highly centralised administrations, such as Sweden, there has been a recent and rapid decentralisation. In the Netherlands, 1993 legislation set in train a process of government deregulation. In Portugal, it has been a policy direction for the last six years. In some countries, such as France for example, there is more caution on account of existing social, cultural and geographical differences.

The question is: What decisions are most appropriate at school level and most acceptable to the public at large? It is clear from the data in Chapter 6 that there are three types of devolved decision-making more favoured than others – school budget, selection of teachers, and teaching methodology. These responses are interesting because they appear to favour school autonomy in methodology but not in subject content or timetable balance, and the selection of teachers but not their pay. They would tend to coincide with national policies in most countries, where there is a simultaneous move towards a national curriculum with school control over delivery, and towards school-based selection of teachers but national pay and conditions.

While preferred forms of school level decision-making are clear and consistent, percentage differences across the board are not so large that they can be ignored or simply taken as endorsement of current or future policy. Indicator C27 (Importance of decision-making at school level) reveals, for example, that a majority of the American public think that schools should have control over everything. A substantial minority in Portugal and the United Kingdom think that schools should choose what subjects to teach, and four out of ten in France think that schools should decide on teachers' salaries and working conditions.

Is this saying, in fact, that many people have little idea of how schools are run and financed and have little insight into the complexities of decision-making? If that is true, is it true for a small or a large number of the population, and does that more knowledgeable portion of the population differ from country to country? So, for example, is it to be expected that countries such as the United States, with a long tradition of local accountability, will have a higher proportion of knowledge among the population than countries which have newly opened such issues to public debate, for example Portugal? Some help in answering this question is available in *Education at a Glance* indicators such as those relating to the country background; breakouts by educational level of respondents and by parents v. non-parents; and the degree to which people in different countries were willing to discriminate between different kinds of decision-making.

There are four countries where the selection and promotion of teachers is ranked significantly above the "item average" for that country – France, the Netherlands, Sweden and the United States. These are interesting because they represent quite different policy history and contemporary practices. It is both long-established policy and practice in the United States, is neither practice nor imminent policy in France, while in the Netherlands and Sweden it is an aspect of developing policy.

Breakouts by educational level reveal some further complex patterns. When all country data are combined, there is a tendency for early school leavers to be more in favour of school level decision-making than late leavers (budgetary matters excepted). However, these overall figures conceal differences between countries. On the item "Teacher selection and promotion" there is, in fact, only one country (France) where there is any significant difference between the "leavers" and "stayers". On "What is taught" and "Time spent on each subject" there are six countries in which there are significant differences between "leavers" and "stayers", and five where there are no significant differences (see Table 6.8). On a country-by-country basis there is one country (the United Kingdom) where there is a significant difference on five of the six categories, and at the other extreme, two countries [Austria and Belgium (Flemish Community)] where there are no significant differences on any of the six items.

The complexity of these patterns does, however, not lend itself to any neat hypotheses and raises perhaps more questions than it answers. For example, does the tendency for people with less schooling to believe that schools should have greater control over what is taught actually reflect that group's lack of knowledge of the working of schools? The fact that this group is also more likely to answer "Not sure" suggests that this may indeed be a factor, but what of the five countries where such differences do *not* exist? What is to be made of the fact that in some countries there are consistently differences by length of formal education and in others consistently no differences? Is it indeed saying something about the relationship between the social structure and the education system in different countries? This set of statistics demands further interpretation, which is best left to Member countries.

In summary, this indicator on the importance of decision-making might be saying that:

- the public in each country has some clear preferences for what is most appropriate for schools to decide themselves (school budget, teacher selection and teaching methods);
- recent public debate in some countries has raised awareness of specific issues; and
- the level of knowledge differs from country to country and within countries.

The questions which are raised by the data may also be saying that an indicator such as this may prove to be useful in two major respects. Firstly, it may raise the issues for debate and inform those issues in an international context. Secondly, it may provide the foundation for a telling set of indicators over time.

9.   Respect for Teachers, and Teachers' Salaries

Public perceptions of respect for teachers are perhaps the most difficult of all the data to interpret but, it might be argued, are an indicator of most concern to policy-makers and the future health of the school system. On what factors does respect for teachers rest: salary; level of qualification; nature or length of training; conditions of service; the difficulty of the job teachers are required to do; comparison with other professions; or on people's own experience of teachers?

Is there a relationship between those who respect teachers and those who use schools, or who directly benefit from schools? Indicators such as national income per capita (C7), educational attainment of the population (C1), entry ratio to higher education (P15) staff employed in education (P9) ratio of students to teaching staff (P10) provide little help in finding associations and correlations with the data from the answers to Question 8 in the questionnaire.

Comparison between groups according to how much schooling they themselves have "consumed" does, however, show significant differences in all but three countries (Austria, Denmark and Spain). After excluding the "Not sure's", in eight countries it is those with *less* schooling who are more inclined to respect teachers. This group does not, however, support higher salaries for teachers (see Question 9) and in four countries there is much stronger support for increased teachers' pay from those with *longer* schooling (Austria, Denmark, Portugal and Spain). Attempts to find explanations for this pattern need to consider the status and salary of other professional groups in each country who are, of course, included in the "longer schooling" group and whose attitudes to salary and respect are shaped accordingly. For example, it might be hypothesised that if less schooling is related to less pay in any given country, then teachers might be seen as well respected, relatively well paid and not in need of any more. If longer schooling is related to membership of professions which are better paid than teaching – medicine, law, accountancy for example – then there might be less respect but a perception of the need for better pay.

In some countries there is a fairly consistent relationship between perceived respect and level of pay. In Austria, for example, teachers are paid relatively well and are relatively well respected. In Sweden, teachers are paid relatively poorly and are rated relatively low in respect. Belgium (Flemish Community), the Netherlands and Portugal are near the mid-point across countries in salary and in respect as well. This is not a consistently strong relationship. However, and if salary is related to respect it is only a partial explanation and not necessarily true for all countries.

Respect for teachers is an indicator whose use will be proved over time. Such a "snapshot" at a given moment may catch a temporary peak or trough. For example, there is evidence to suggest that the status of teachers in the United States has been progressively rising since bottoming out in 1983 (Snyder and Hoffman, 1993). The relatively low rating in Spain may reflect a sudden spurt in recruitment over a short period to meet the demands of the educational explosion and the high-profile public debate on educational reform. It is yet another reminder that interpretation requires a measured approach rather than an approach which simply measures.

Conclusion

by

Archie McGlynn

Her Majesty's Chief Inspector of Schools,
Scottish Office Education Department, Edinburgh, Scotland

It has been demonstrated that beneath the variation of policy and practice from one country to the next, lie common concerns which seem to be integral to the provision of public education. The recognition of these underlying similarities was a useful starting point from which to explore and identify key questions in the search for common indicators of educational performance across a range of countries.

This report, together with the network's technical report (Bosker, 1995), illuminates the way in which an international survey proceeds through various phases. These may be characterised as: conceptual; political; technical; and developmental.

Conceptual issues figured large in the early stages of the network. The founding Member countries had to agree on what they were there for and where, jointly, they wished to go. This involved clarification of terminology, concepts, assumptions and differing cultural understandings. *Political issues* were always on the agenda but at most times in the background. Most members brought with them a consciousness of political priorities and policy-making in their own countries and were generally able to predict or pre-empt possible reactions. These political issues came into the foreground of discussion at specific times – for example, on the funding of surveys, the selection of questionnaire items, and the ownership and use of survey findings. There was, however, very little political friction. On the whole, Member countries were swift to agree to the financing of the survey, and ready to agree to the release of data to the OECD on the basis of certain assurances. *Technical issues* became the focus in the latter stages when attention turned to the production of indicators. Discussion in the network meetings centred on issues such as standardisation of methodology and sampling, statistical reliability and validity, selection and presentation of indicators. What might be called *developmental issues* were those which had to do with the rationale of the network, its mission and its intended development. It was a learning experience for all its members, but there was also a whole which became greater than the sum of its parts. In other words, the network became the repository and source of new knowledge and expertise. As countries joined the network at successive stages they also had to come to terms with the history of the network and to make their own place within its future.

The network has expressed the hope that its work will lead to increased support for indicators of attitudes and customer satisfaction in the domain of education. Members believe, as stated by Michel and MacBeath in Chapter 3 of this report, that "attitudes, values and opinions are in fact a major element of how the education system actually works, and that the effectiveness of the system rests on people's motivation, satisfaction and sense of commitment".

In his review of *Education at a Glance* (OECD, 1993), Moser argued "that it is vital in our various countries, to get the general public interested in, and committed to, education". The new indicators and activities of Network D are a recognition that the general public are stakeholders in education. In the same way, Orivel urged the OECD "to consider relatively simple and not too costly opinion surveys in order to compare the attitudes of different groups concerning the national education system, its successes and its failures, its advantages and its drawbacks". Network D's seven indicators and this report represent a first step towards that objective; a model has been built with a distinctive approach capable of taking the next steps.

Conclusion

par

Archie McGlynn
Inspecteur en chef des écoles,
Département de l'Éducation du Scottish Office, Edimbourg, Écosse

Le rapport du réseau ainsi que son rapport technique (Bosker, 1995) montrent comment une enquête internationale passe par diverses phases de croissance à mesure qu'elle se rapproche de son objectif à différents points du cycle de vie du réseau. Ces différentes phases sont les suivantes : conception théorique, niveau politique, niveau technique et développement.

Les problèmes théoriques ont occupé une grande place aux premiers stades d'activité du réseau. Il a fallu déblayer le terrain au niveau de la terminologie et des concepts, des hypothèses et des différences culturelles. La plupart des membres avaient, au départ, une certaine conscience des priorités politiques et des modes d'élaboration d'une politique dans leur propre pays et ils ont été généralement à même de prévoir ou de prévenir d'éventuelles réactions. Ces questions politiques ont été abordées à certains moments lors des débats, par exemple à propos de la question du financement des enquêtes, de la sélection des rubriques de questionnaire, de la propriété et de l'utilisation des conclusions des enquêtes. Les frictions politiques ont cependant été très limitées. Les questions techniques ne sont venues au premier plan qu'à un stade ultérieur, à propos de l'élaboration d'indicateurs. Sur le fond, les débats au sein du réseau ont porté sur des questions telles que la normalisation des méthodes et des sondages, la fiabilité et la validité des statistiques, ainsi que le choix et la présentation des indicateurs. Ce que l'on pourrait appeler les questions de développement ont concerné la raison d'être du réseau, sa mission et son développement prévu. Tous les membres du réseau ont eu la possibilité d'apprendre, mais par ailleurs, le tout est devenu plus grand que la somme de ses parties. En d'autres termes, le réseau est devenu le dépositaire et la source de connaissances et de compétences nouvelles.

Le réseau D espère que son travail aboutira à un soutien accru à des indicateurs d'attitude et de satisfaction dans le domaine de l'éducation. Le réseau considère que les attitudes, les valeurs et les opinions constituent un élément majeur du mode de fonctionnement effectif des systèmes éducatifs et que l'efficacité de ceux-ci dépend de la motivation et de la satisfaction des intéressés et de leur attachement au système en question. Dans leur étude sur *Regards sur l'éducation* (OCDE, 1993), Moser et Orivel ont instamment demandé à l'OCDE d'envisager d'entreprendre des enquêtes pour connaître les vues du public et d'autres protagonistes. Les sept indicateurs du Réseau D et ce rapport constituent un premier pas important vers la réalisation de cet objectif ; on a établi un modèle caractérisé par une approche originale, capable de passer aux stades suivants.

References/Références

BALLION, R. (1991), ''The importance of opinion study in the education system'', in OECD (ed.), *Making Education Count. Developing and using international indicators,* OECD, Paris.

BLANKEN, van, M.A., and BOSKER, R. (1993), *Attitudes and Expectations towards Education: The Construction of a Dutch Version of an International Questionnaire,* University of Twente, Enschede.

BOSKER, R. (1995), ''INES technical document'', OECD, Paris.

BOTTANI, N. and TUIJNMAN, A. (1994), ''International education indicators: framework, development and interpretation'', in OECD (ed.), *Making Education Count. Developing and Using International Indicators,* OECD, Paris.

BOURDIEU, P. (1977), *Reproduction in Education Society and Culture,* Sage Publications, Newbury Park, CA.

BRADBURN, N.M. and GILFORD, D.M. (1990), *A Framework and Principles for International Comparative Studies in Education,* National Research Council, National Academy Press, Washington, DC.

BROOKOVER, W. *et al.* (1979), *School Social Systems and Student Achievement,* Praeger, New York.

CAIRNEY, T.H., and MUNSIE, L. (1992), *Beyond Tokenism: Parents as Partners in Literacy,* University of Western Australia.

COCHRAN, W.G. (1977), *Sampling Techniques,* John Wiley and Sons, New York.

HM Inspectors of Schools (1992), *Using Ethos Indicators in Secondary School Self-Evaluation,* Scottish Office Education Department, Edinburgh, Scotland.

HUTMACHER, W. and GROS, D. (1994), *Expectations, Priorities and Attitudes with Regard to the School,* Univox ID – Education, Copyright EFS and SRS, Geneva.

MACBEATH, J. (1991), ''Common concerns and the search for indicators (Préoccupations communes)'', A bilingual summary report of the Network D discussions in the Hague in February 1991, Scottish Office Education Department, Edinburgh, Scotland.

MACBEATH, J. and TURNER, M. (1990), *Learning out of School: Homework, Policy and Practice,* Jordanhill College, Glasgow, and Scottish Office Education Department, Edinburgh, Scotland.

MACBEATH, J., VAN RIE, T., and LEYSEN, A. (1991), *Towards Attitudinal Indicators – A Survey of Surveys Phase 2: The Report of Network D,* November, Scottish Office Education Department, Edinburgh, Scotland.

MERTTENS, R. and HANNON, P. (1993), *Conditions of Learning at Home and in School,* University of North London Institute of Education, London.

MICHEL, A. (1993), "Le pilotage d'un système complexe: l'Éducation nationale", *Revue Administration et Éducation*, No. 2, Paris.

MORTIMORE, P., SAMMONS, P., STOLL, L., LWIS, D., and ECOB, R. (1988), *School Matters: The Junior Years*, Open Books, Wells, United Kingdom.

MURRAY, C.A. *et al.,* (1990), "The emerging British underclass", *Choice in Welfare Series*, Vol. 2, Institute of Education, London.

MVA Consultancy and MACBEATH, J. (1989), *Talking about Schools*, Scottish Office Education Department, Edinburgh, Scotland.

OECD (1992), *Education at a Glance: OECD Indicators* (bilingual), 1st edition, CERI, Paris.

OECD (1993), *Education at a Glance: OECD Indicators* (bilingual), 2nd edition, CERI, Paris.

OECD (1995), *Education at a Glance: OECD Indicators*, 3rd edition, CERI, Paris.

POSTLETHWAITE, T.N. and WILEY, D. (1992), *The IEA Study of Science II,* Pergamon Press, Oxford.

ROBITAILLE, D. and GARDEN, R. (1989), *The IEA Study of Mathematics II*, Pergamon Press, Oxford.

SCHEERENS, J. (1992), *Effective Schooling: Research, Theory and Practice, School Effectiveness and School Improvement,* Cassell, London.

SCHUBAUER-LEONI, M. L. (1991), "Indicateurs internationaux de l'éducation dans le domaine des attentes et attitudes", unpublished report, University of Geneva, Geneva.

SCHUBAUER-LEONI, M.L. (1992), "Conceptual framework: attitude indicators", unpublished report, University of Geneva, Geneva.

SNYDER T. and HOFFMAN C. (1993), *Digest of Education Statistics*, National Center for Education Statistics, Washington, DC.

US National Commission on Excellence in Education (1983), *A Nation at Risk: The Imperative for Educational Reform*, Government Printing Office, Washington, DC.

WALBERG, H. (1985), "Evaluation in education", *Educational Leadership*, Vol. 7, Pergamon and Elsevier, United Kingdom.

Network D's Indicators in *Education at a Glance* (OECD, 1995)
Tableaux des indicateurs du Réseau D
dans Regards sur l'éducation *(OCDE, 1995)*

Indicator C21:   Importance of subjects
Indicator C22:   Importance of qualities/aptitudes
Indicator C23:   Confidence in the teaching of subjects and development of qualities
Indicator C24:   Home/School balance for the personal and social development of young people
Indicator C25:   Respect for secondary teachers
Indicator C26:   Priorities in school practice
Indicator C27:   Importance of decision-making at school-level

Table/Tableau C21.

Percentage of respondents who thought the subjects were "essential" or "very important"

(1993/94)

Pourcentage des répondants qui estimaient que les matières suivantes étaient «essentielles» ou «très importantes»

	Physical education	The arts	The sciences	Foreign languages	Native (school) language	Social subjects (e.g. history, geography)	Mathematics	Education for citizenship	Technology	Information technology (e.g. computing)	Subject average within each country
Austria	73	43	67	91	92	72	92	64	60	79	**73.2**
Belgium (Flemish Com.)	63	29	57	88	86	44	80	66	53	77	**64.3**
Denmark	38	36	46	79	85	41	81	46	:	56	**56.4**
Finland	61	31	53	87	77	49	84	35	39	71	**58.9**
France	50	31	63	87	97	69	88	67	47	69	**66.8**
Netherlands	41	31	64	85	90	47	69	41	42	75	**58.6**
Portugal	71	55	76	85	91	75	86	73	66	76	**75.5**
Spain	52	44	65	72	67	66	73	66	63	66	**63.4**
Sweden	54	31	65	87	94	58	91	70	38	63	**65.0**
Switzerland	67	58	63	77	84	62	82	65	52	71	**68.1**
United Kingdom	41	26	66	56	88	50	93	36	57	72	**58.4**
United States	62	47	85	53	92	80	96	77	36	86	**71.3**
Country average for each subject	**56.0**	**38.4**	**64.1**	**79.0**	**86.9**	**59.5**	**84.6**	**59.0**	**50.3**	**71.6**	

Source: OECD (1995).

130

Table/Tableau C22.

Percentage of respondents who thought the following qualities were "essential" or "very important"

(1993/94)

Pourcentage des répondants qui estimaient que les qualités suivantes étaient «essentielles» ou «très importantes»

	Self-confidence	How to live among people from different backgrounds	A desire to continue studies or training	An understanding of other countries of the world	Skills and knowledge which will help to get a job	Skills and knowledge which will help to continue studies or training	A lifestyle which promotes good health	Being a good citizen	Qualities average within each country
Austria	93	83	79	71	92	88	83	68	**82.3**
Belgium (Flemish Com.)	90	81	75	61	85	78	78	80	**78.5**
Denmark	87	84	65	61	75	70	61	63	**70.6**
Finland	89	87	68	62	82	76	77	76	**77.1**
France	93	83	87	64	91	84	85	82	**83.5**
Netherlands	90	85	73	63	80	83	61	65	**74.8**
Portugal	82	82	81	71	85	85	86	87	**82.6**
Spain	75	73	70	65	77	73	72	75	**72.5**
Sweden	90	75	68	61	85	80	72	76	**75.9**
Switzerland	93	88	76	74	89	86	79	58	**80.4**
United Kingdom	89	73	69	49	91	..	72	82	**75.1**
United States	89	82	88	67	94	90	83	86	**84.8**
Country average for each quality	**88.4**	**81.3**	**74.8**	**64.2**	**85.5**	**81.2**	**75.7**	**74.9**	

Source: OECD (1995).

Table/Tableau C23.

**Percentage of respondents who viewed subjects as important
and who thought they were taught well, and percentage of respondents
who thought qualities were important and that they were developed well**

(1993/94)

*Pourcentage des répondants qui estimaient que les matières étaient importantes
et qu'elles étaient bien enseignées, et pourcentage des répondants qui estimaient
que les qualités étaient importantes et que leur acquisition était favorisée*

	Average confidence in important subjects	Average confidence in important qualities
Austria	78	63
Belgium (Flemish Community)	72	58
Denmark	75	69
Finland	77	55
France	84	62
Netherlands	64	51
Portugal	58	58
Spain	46	37
Sweden	40	18
Switzerland	76	63
United Kingdom	63	47
United States	63	59
Country average	**66.2**	**53.4**

Source: OECD (1995).

Table/Tableau C24.

Percentage of people who answered how much responsibility they thought the home should have compared to school for the personal and social development of young people

(1993/94)

Pourcentage de la population qui a répondu à la question sur la responsabilité que la famille devrait avoir par rapport à l'établissement scolaire en ce qui concerne l'épanouissement personnel et social des jeunes

	Home should have more responsibility than the school	Home should share responsibility equally with the school	Home should have less responsibility than the school
Austria	42	55	3
Belgium (Flemish Community)	28	65	7
Denmark	55	43	2
Finland	55	44	1
France	14	79	7
Netherlands	44	53	3
Portugal	18	67	14
Spain	15	80	5
Sweden	38	60	2
United Kingdom	14	81	5
United States	34	63	3
Country average	**32.5**	**62.8**	**4.7**

Source: OECD (1995).

Table/Tableau C25.

Different levels of respect for teachers as professionals

(percentage, 1993/94)

Différents niveaux de considération pour les enseignants en tant que professionnels

	Very respected	Fairly respected	Very and fairly respected	Not very respected	Not at all respected	Not sure
Austria	18	57	74	18	3	4
Belgium (Flemish Community)	8	56	64	29	6	2
Denmark	7	52	59	35	2	3
Finland	7	51	58	40	2	..
France	8	47	55	35	9	2
Netherlands	5	55	61	33	2	4
Portugal	12	47	59	13	3	25
Spain	3	29	32	49	9	10
Sweden	7	40	48	37	6	9
United Kingdom	7	49	56	32	6	7
United States	20	48	68	24	5	3
Country average	**9.3**	**48.3**	**57.6**	**31.3**	**4.8**	**6.9**

Source: OECD (1995).

Table/Tableau C26.

Percentage of respondents who thought it is "essential" and "very important" for schools to emphasise the following practices in order to achieve their goals

(1993/94)

Pourcentage des répondants qui estimaient "essentiel" ou "très important" que les écoles s'attachent aux aspects suivants pour s'acquitter de leur mission

	Careers advice and guidance	Helping with difficulties in learning	Strong leadership from the head teacher	Maintaining discipline	Regular homework	A wide range of different subjects taught	Keeping parents well informed and involved	School practices average within each country
Austria	93	92	47	73	57	70	86	**73.9**
Belgium (Flemish Community)	76	92	73	81	58	74	85	**76.9**
Denmark	66	81	46	56	39	51	74	**59.1**
Finland	74	89	42	91	71	29	72	**66.8**
France	93	94	82	89	57	70	76	**80.3**
Netherlands	81	92	61	69	60	67	83	**73.4**
Portugal	81	87	69	79	67	38	87	**72.6**
Spain	71	76	38	60	39	55	74	**58.9**
Sweden	77	88	62	79	49	48	80	**69.1**
Switzerland	82	92	56	67	52	71	88	**72.5**
United Kingdom	85	94	75	90	63	70	87	**80.5**
United States	84	92	85	93	78	79	95	**86.6**
Country average for each school practice	**80.2**	**89.1**	**61.4**	**77.1**	**57.5**	**60.2**	**82.3**	

Source: OECD (1995).

134

Table/Tableau C27.

Percentage of respondents who thought it was "very important" for decisions to be made by schools themselves
(1993/94)

Pourcentage des répondants qui estimaient qu'il est «très important» que les décisions soient prises par les établissements scolaires eux-mêmes

	What subjects are taught	How subjects are taught	Amount of time spent teaching each subject	How the school budget is spent	Teacher selection and promotion	Teachers' salaries and working conditions	Items average within each country
Austria	31	36	28	33	31	18	29.6
Belgium (Flemish Community)	22	41	27	36	39	26	31.9
Denmark	20	32	16	34	31	12	24.0
Finland	18	35	26	40	34	22	28.9
France	34	56	51	50	59	43	48.7
Netherlands	15	35	22	31	47	24	28.9
Portugal	44	55	50	56	51	37	48.8
Spain	13	19	17	19	20	13	16.9
Sweden	23	38	24	51	44	17	32.8
Switzerland	18	32	21	22	26	14	22.0
United Kingdom	39	50	44	57	50	32	45.3
United States	53	60	57	64	67	57	59.8
Country average for each item	**27.7**	**40.6**	**31.8**	**41.0**	**41.6**	**26.2**	

Source: OECD (1995).

Network D's Survey Questionnaire, 2 April 1993
The general public's expectations of, and confidence in, education

Questionnaire d'enquête du Réseau D, 2 avril 1993
Attentes et attitude de l'opinion publique vis-à-vis de l'enseignement

Q.1. The following are eleven examples of things that young people study or could study in secondary school. In your view how important are each of these?

	Essential	Very important	Fairly important	Not very important	Not at all important	Not sure either way
Physical education						
The Arts (*e.g.* music, fine art)						
The Sciences (*e.g.* chemistry, biology, physics)						
Foreign languages						
Language and literature*						
Social subjects (*e.g.* history, geography)						
Mathematics						
Education for citizenship ("civic" or "social educ.")						
Technology/technical studies						
Information technology (*e.g.* computing)						
Religious studies #						

* Put in native language here *e.g.* English, French.
# Optional.

Q.2. In your view how confident are you that schools are teaching these well?

	Very confident	Fairly confident	Not very confident	Not at all confident	Not sure either way
Physical education					
The Arts (*e.g.* music, fine art)					
The Sciences (*e.g.* chemistry, biology, physics)					
Foreign languages					
Language and literature*					
Social subjects (*e.g.* history, geography)					
Mathematics					
Education for citizenship ("civic" or "social educ.")					
Technology/technical studies					
Information technology (*e.g.* computing)					
Religious studies #					

* Put in native language here *e.g.* English, French.
\# Optional.

Q.3. The following are qualities ♦ that young people may have developed by the end of their compulsory schooling*. In your view how important is it that schools aim to develop such qualities?

	Essential	Very important	Fairly important	Not very important	Not at all important	Not sure either way
Self-confidence						
How to live among other people from different backgrounds						
A desire to continue studies or training						
An understanding of other countries of the world						
Skills and knowledge which will help to get a job						
Skills and knowledge which will help to continue studies or training						
A lifestyle which promotes good health						
Being a good citizen						
# Gaining qualifications o						

♦ Where it is essential for translation purposes, words to indicate ability/capability could be added in parenthesis here.
* School leaving age in relevant country.
# Optional.
o Or a formulation of words to indicate the meaning of ''having a piece of paper in one's hand''.

Q.4. How confident are you that schools in general actually do have a major effect on the development of these qualities ◆?

	Very confident	Fairly confident	Not very confident	Not at all confident	Not sure either way
Self-confidence					
How to live among people from different backgrounds					
A desire to continue studies or training					
An understanding of other countries of the world					
Skills and knowledge which will help to get a job					
Skills and knowledge which will help to continue studies or training					
A lifestyle which promotes good health					
Being a good citizen					
#Gaining qualifications o					

◆ Where it is essential for translation purposes, words to indicate ability/capability could be added in parenthesis here.
\# Optional.
o Or a formulation of words to indicate the meaning of ''having a piece of paper in one's hand''.

Q.5. In your view how important are each of the following for schools to emphasise in order to achieve their goals?

	Essential	Very important	Fairly important	Not very important	Not at all important	Not sure either way
Careers advice and guidance						
Helping with difficulties in learning						
Strong leadership from the headteacher o						
Maintaining discipline						
Regular homework						
A wide range of different subjects taught						
Keeping parents well informed and involved						

o This word to indicate the person (or persons) at the head of, in charge of, the school.

Q.6. How much responsibility do you think the school should have (compared with the home) for the personal and social development of young people?

The main responsibility	
Shared equally with the home	
Less responsibility than the home	

141

Q.7. In your view how important is it that the following decisions are made by the individual school itself?

	Very important	Fairly important	Not very important	Not at all important	Not sure either way
What subjects are taught					
How subjects are taught					
Amount of time spent teaching each subject					
How the school budget is spent					
Teacher selection and promotion					
Teachers' salaries and working conditions					

Q.8. In your view[1] how respected are secondary teachers[2] as a profession?[3]

Very respected	
Fairly respected	
Not very respected	
Not at all respected	
Not sure either way	

1. The question is to get at what the respondent thinks that other people think.
2. The group of teachers which is the focus of the question is the group of teachers who teach the stage defined as the last years of compulsory education.
3. The question is to get at what the respondent thinks about teachers as people, rather than as a profession.

Optional Question

Q.9. Do you think teachers[1] should earn more or less than they do now?

Earn much more	
Earn a little more	
Earn the same	
Earn a little less	
Earn a lot less	
Not sure either way	

1. The same group of teachers is implied in Q.8.

List of Contributors

Archie McGlynn (Chair)	HM Chief Inspector of Schools, Scottish Office Education Department, Edinburgh, Scotland
John MacBeath	The Quality in Education Centre, University of Strathclyde, Glasgow, Scotland
Roel Bosker	Department of Education, University of Twente, the Netherlands
Birgitte Bovin	Ministry of Education, Denmark
Carol Calvert	HM Inspectors of Schools, Scottish Office Education Department, Edinburgh, Scotland
Carmen Castanhiera	Department for Programming and Financial Management, Ministry of Education, Portugal
Maija-Leena Clarkson	National Board of Education, Finland
Frans Daems	Department of Didactics, University of Antwerp, the Netherlands
Ronald Delémont	Swiss Federal Statistical Office, Switzerland
Jan van Dommelen	Ministry of Education, Culture and Science, the Netherlands
Lillian King	Pelavin Research Institute, United States
Agnes Leysen	Department of Didactics, University of Antwerp, the Netherlands
Consuelo Vélaz de Medrano	Cabinet of the Secretariat of State, Department of Education and Science, Spain
Alain Michel	Department of National Education, France
Mats Myrberg	National Agency for Education, Sweden
Paul Planchon	National Center for Education Statistics, United States
Laura Salganik	Pelavin Research Institute, United States
Erich Svecnik	Centre for School Development of the Federal Ministry of Education and the Arts (Evaluation and School Research), Austria
Roger Thomas	Social Community and Planning Research, United Kingdom

ÉGALEMENT DISPONIBLES

Regards sur l'éducation - Les indicateurs de l'OCDE
FF 220   FFE 285   £35   US$ 54   DM 83

OECD Education Statistics, 1985-1992/Statistiques de l'enseignement de l'OCDE, 1985-1992 (bilingue)
FF 160   FFE 210   £25   US$ 40   DM 60

Measuring the Quality of Schools/Mesurer la qualité des établissements scolaires (bilingue)
FF 120   FFE 155   £20   US$ 29   DM 47

Measuring What Students Learn/Mesurer les résultats scolaires (bilingue)
FF 110   FFE 140   £17   US$ 27   DM 40

Education and Employment/Formation et emploi (bilingue)
FF 90   FFE 115   £14   US$ 22   DM 34

Les processus de décision dans 14 systèmes éducatifs de l'OCDE (à paraître prochainement)

MAIN SALES OUTLETS OF OECD PUBLICATIONS
PRINCIPAUX POINTS DE VENTE DES PUBLICATIONS DE L'OCDE

ARGENTINA – ARGENTINE
Carlos Hirsch S.R.L.
Galería Güemes, Florida 165, 4° Piso
1333 Buenos Aires   Tel. (1) 331.1787 y 331.2391
Telefax: (1) 331.1787

AUSTRALIA – AUSTRALIE
D.A. Information Services
648 Whitehorse Road, P.O.B 163
Mitcham, Victoria 3132   Tel. (03) 873.4411
Telefax: (03) 873.5679

AUSTRIA – AUTRICHE
Gerold & Co.
Graben 31
Wien I   Tel. (0222) 533.50.14

BELGIUM – BELGIQUE
Jean De Lannoy
Avenue du Roi 202
B-1060 Bruxelles   Tel. (02) 538.51.69/538.08.41
Telefax: (02) 538.08.41

CANADA
Renouf Publishing Company Ltd.
1294 Algoma Road
Ottawa, ON K1B 3W8   Tel. (613) 741.4333
Telefax: (613) 741.5439
Stores:
61 Sparks Street
Ottawa, ON K1P 5R1   Tel. (613) 238.8985
211 Yonge Street
Toronto, ON M5B 1M4   Tel. (416) 363.3171
Telefax: (416)363.59.63
Les Éditions La Liberté Inc.
3020 Chemin Sainte-Foy
Sainte-Foy, PQ G1X 3V6   Tel. (418) 658.3763
Telefax: (418) 658.3763
Federal Publications Inc.
165 University Avenue, Suite 701
Toronto, ON M5H 3B8   Tel. (416) 860.1611
Telefax: (416) 860.1608
Les Publications Fédérales
1185 Université
Montréal, QC H3B 3A7   Tel. (514) 954.1633
Telefax : (514) 954.1635

CHINA – CHINE
China National Publications Import
Export Corporation (CNPIEC)
16 Gongti E. Road, Chaoyang District
P.O. Box 88 or 50
Beijing 100704 PR   Tel. (01) 506.6688
Telefax: (01) 506.3101

CZECH REPUBLIC – RÉPUBLIQUE TCHÈQUE
Artia Pegas Press Ltd.
Narodni Trida 25
POB 825
111 21 Praha 1   Tel. 26.65.68
Telefax: 26.20.81

DENMARK – DANEMARK
Munksgaard Book and Subscription Service
35, Nørre Søgade, P.O. Box 2148
DK-1016 København K   Tel. (33) 12.85.70
Telefax: (33) 12.93.87

EGYPT – ÉGYPTE
Middle East Observer
41 Sherif Street
Cairo   Tel. 392.6919
Telefax: 360-6804

FINLAND – FINLANDE
Akateeminen Kirjakauppa
Keskuskatu 1, P.O. Box 128
00100 Helsinki
Subscription Services/Agence d'abonnements :
P.O. Box 23
00371 Helsinki   Tel. (358 0) 12141
Telefax: (358 0) 121.4450

FRANCE
OECD/OCDE
Mail Orders/Commandes par correspondance:
2, rue André-Pascal
75775 Paris Cedex 16   Tel. (33-1) 45.24.82.00
Telefax: (33-1) 49.10.42.76
Telex: 640048 OCDE
Orders via Minitel, France only/
Commandes par Minitel, France exclusivement :
36 15 OCDE

OECD Bookshop/Librairie de l'OCDE :
33, rue Octave-Feuillet
75016 Paris   Tel. (33-1) 45.24.81.67
(33-1) 45.24.81.81
Documentation Française
29, quai Voltaire
75007 Paris   Tel. 40.15.70.00
Gibert Jeune (Droit-Économie)
6, place Saint-Michel
75006 Paris   Tel. 43.25.91.19
Librairie du Commerce International
10, avenue d'Iéna
75016 Paris   Tel. 40.73.34.60
Librairie Dunod
Université Paris-Dauphine
Place du Maréchal de Lattre de Tassigny
75016 Paris   Tel. (1) 44.05.40.13
Librairie Lavoisier
11, rue Lavoisier
75008 Paris   Tel. 42.65.39.95
Librairie L.G.D.J. - Montchrestien
20, rue Soufflot
75005 Paris   Tel. 46.33.89.85
Librairie des Sciences Politiques
30, rue Saint-Guillaume
75007 Paris   Tel. 45.48.36.02
P.U.F.
49, boulevard Saint-Michel
75005 Paris   Tel. 43.25.83.40
Librairie de l'Université
12a, rue Nazareth
13100 Aix-en-Provence   Tel. (16) 42.26.18.08
Documentation Française
165, rue Garibaldi
69003 Lyon   Tel. (16) 78.63.32.23
Librairie Decitre
29, place Bellecour
69002 Lyon   Tel. (16) 72.40.54.54

GERMANY – ALLEMAGNE
OECD Publications and Information Centre
August-Bebel-Allee 6
D-53175 Bonn   Tel. (0228) 959.120
Telefax: (0228) 959.12.17

GREECE – GRÈCE
Librairie Kauffmann
Mavrokordatou 9
106 78 Athens   Tel. (01) 32.55.321
Telefax: (01) 36.33.967

HONG-KONG
Swindon Book Co. Ltd.
13–15 Lock Road
Kowloon, Hong Kong   Tel. 2376.2062
Telefax: 2376.0685

HUNGARY – HONGRIE
Euro Info Service
Margitsziget, Európa Ház
1138 Budapest   Tel. (1) 111.62.16
Telefax : (1) 111.60.61

ICELAND – ISLANDE
Mál Mog Menning
Laugavegi 18, Pósthólf 392
121 Reykjavik   Tel. 162.35.23

INDIA – INDE
Oxford Book and Stationery Co.
Scindia House
New Delhi 110001   Tel.(11) 331.5896/5308
Telefax: (11) 332.5993
17 Park Street
Calcutta 700016   Tel. 240832

INDONESIA – INDONÉSIE
Pdii-Lipi
P.O. Box 4298
Jakarta 12042   Tel. (21) 573.34.67
Telefax: (21) 573.34.67

IRELAND – IRLANDE
Government Supplies Agency
Publications Section
4/5 Harcourt Road
Dublin 2   Tel. 661.31.11
Telefax: 478.06.45

ISRAEL
Praedicta
5 Shatner Street
P.O. Box 34030
Jerusalem 91430   Tel. (2) 52.84.90/1/2
Telefax: (2) 52.84.93
R.O.Y.
P.O. Box 13056
Tel Aviv 61130   Tél. (3) 49.61.08
Telefax (3) 544.60.39

ITALY – ITALIE
Libreria Commissionaria Sansoni
Via Duca di Calabria 1/1
50125 Firenze   Tel. (055) 64.54.15
Telefax: (055) 64.12.57
Via Bartolini 29
20155 Milano   Tel. (02) 36.50.83
Editrice e Libreria Herder
Piazza Montecitorio 120
00186 Roma   Tel. 679.46.28
Telefax: 678.47.51
Libreria Hoepli
Via Hoepli 5
20121 Milano   Tel. (02) 86.54.46
Telefax: (02) 805.28.86
Libreria Scientifica
Dott. Lucio de Biasio 'Aeiou'
Via Coronelli, 6
20146 Milano   Tel. (02) 48.95.45.52
Telefax: (02) 48.95.45.48

JAPAN – JAPON
OECD Publications and Information Centre
Landic Akasaka Building
2-3-4 Akasaka, Minato-ku
Tokyo 107   Tel. (81.3) 3586.2016
Telefax: (81.3) 3584.7929

KOREA – CORÉE
Kyobo Book Centre Co. Ltd.
P.O. Box 1658, Kwang Hwa Moon
Seoul   Tel. 730.78.91
Telefax: 735.00.30

MALAYSIA – MALAISIE
University of Malaya Bookshop
University of Malaya
P.O. Box 1127, Jalan Pantai Baru
59700 Kuala Lumpur
Malaysia   Tel. 756.5000/756.5425
Telefax: 756.3246

MEXICO – MEXIQUE
Revistas y Periodicos Internacionales S.A. de C.V.
Florencia 57 - 1004
Mexico, D.F. 06600   Tel. 207.81.00
Telefax : 208.39.79

NETHERLANDS – PAYS-BAS
SDU Uitgeverij Plantijnstraat
Externe Fondsen
Postbus 20014
2500 EA's-Gravenhage   Tel. (070) 37.89.880
Voor bestellingen: Telefax: (070) 34.75.778

NEW ZEALAND
NOUVELLE-ZÉLANDE
Legislation Services
P.O. Box 12418
Thorndon, Wellington   Tel. (04) 496.5652
                           Telefax: (04) 496.5698

NORWAY – NORVÈGE
Narvesen Info Center – NIC
Bertrand Narvesens vei 2
P.O. Box 6125 Etterstad
0602 Oslo 6   Tel. (022) 57.33.00
                  Telefax: (022) 68.19.01

PAKISTAN
Mirza Book Agency
65 Shahrah Quaid-E-Azam
Lahore 54000   Tel. (42) 353.601
                   Telefax: (42) 231.730

PHILIPPINE – PHILIPPINES
International Book Center
5th Floor, Filipinas Life Bldg.
Ayala Avenue
Metro Manila   Tel. 81.96.76
                   Telex 23312 RHP PH

PORTUGAL
Livraria Portugal
Rua do Carmo 70-74
Apart. 2681
1200 Lisboa   Tel.: (01) 347.49.82/5
                  Telefax: (01) 347.02.64

SINGAPORE – SINGAPOUR
Gower Asia Pacific Pte Ltd.
Golden Wheel Building
41, Kallang Pudding Road, No. 04-03
Singapore 1334   Tel. 741.5166
                     Telefax: 742.9356

SPAIN – ESPAGNE
Mundi-Prensa Libros S.A.
Castelló 37, Apartado 1223
Madrid 28001   Tel. (91) 431.33.99
                   Telefax: (91) 575.39.98

Libreria Internacional AEDOS
Consejo de Ciento 391
08009 – Barcelona   Tel. (93) 488.30.09
                        Telefax: (93) 487.76.59
Llibreria de la Generalitat
Palau Moja
Rambla dels Estudis, 118
08002 – Barcelona
            (Subscripcions) Tel. (93) 318.80.12
            (Publicacions) Tel. (93) 302.67.23
            Telefax: (93) 412.18.54

SRI LANKA
Centre for Policy Research
c/o Colombo Agencies Ltd.
No. 300-304, Galle Road
Colombo 3   Tel. (1) 574240, 573551-2
                Telefax: (1) 575394, 510711

SWEDEN – SUÈDE
Fritzes Information Center
Box 16356
Regeringsgatan 12
106 47 Stockholm   Tel. (08) 690.90.90
                       Telefax: (08) 20.50.21

Subscription Agency/Agence d'abonnements :
Wennergren-Williams Info AB
P.O. Box 1305
171 25 Solna   Tel. (08) 705.97.50
                   Téléfax : (08) 27.00.71

SWITZERLAND – SUISSE
Maditec S.A. (Books and Periodicals - Livres
et périodiques)
Chemin des Palettes 4
Case postale 266
1020 Renens VD 1   Tel. (021) 635.08.65
                       Telefax: (021) 635.07.80

Librairie Payot S.A.
4, place Pépinet
CP 3212
1002 Lausanne   Tel. (021) 341.33.47
                    Telefax: (021) 341.33.45

Librairie Unilivres
6, rue de Candolle
1205 Genève   Tel. (022) 320.26.23
                  Telefax: (022) 329.73.18

Subscription Agency/Agence d'abonnements :
Dynapresse Marketing S.A.
38 avenue Vibert
1227 Carouge   Tel.: (022) 308.07.89
                   Telefax: (022) 308.07.99

See also – Voir aussi :
OECD Publications and Information Centre
August-Bebel-Allee 6
D-53175 Bonn (Germany)   Tel. (0228) 959.120
                             Telefax: (0228) 959.12.17

TAIWAN – FORMOSE
Good Faith Worldwide Int'l. Co. Ltd.
9th Floor, No. 118, Sec. 2
Chung Hsiao E. Road
Taipei   Tel. (02) 391.7396/391.7397
             Telefax: (02) 394.9176

THAILAND – THAÏLANDE
Suksit Siam Co. Ltd.
113, 115 Fuang Nakhon Rd.
Opp. Wat Rajbopith
Bangkok 10200   Tel. (662) 225.9531/2
                    Telefax: (662) 222.5188

TURKEY – TURQUIE
Kültür Yayinlari Is-Türk Ltd. Sti.
Atatürk Bulvari No. 191/Kat 13
Kavaklidere/Ankara   Tel. 428.11.40 Ext. 2458
Dolmabahce Cad. No. 29
Besiktas/Istanbul   Tel. 260.71.88
                        Telex: 43482B

UNITED KINGDOM – ROYAUME-UNI
HMSO
Gen. enquiries   Tel. (071) 873 0011
Postal orders only:
P.O. Box 276, London SW8 5DT
Personal Callers HMSO Bookshop
49 High Holborn, London WC1V 6HB
                     Telefax: (071) 873 8200
Branches at: Belfast, Birmingham, Bristol, Edin-
burgh, Manchester

UNITED STATES – ÉTATS-UNIS
OECD Publications and Information Centre
2001 L Street N.W., Suite 700
Washington, D.C. 20036-4910 Tel. (202) 785.6323
                            Telefax: (202) 785.0350

VENEZUELA
Libreria del Este
Avda F. Miranda 52, Aptdo. 60337
Edificio Galipán
Caracas 106   Tel. 951.1705/951.2307/951.1297
                  Telegram: Libreste Caracas

Subscription to OECD periodicals may also be
placed through main subscription agencies.

Les abonnements aux publications périodiques de
l'OCDE peuvent être souscrits auprès des
principales agences d'abonnement.

Orders and inquiries from countries where Distribu-
tors have not yet been appointed should be sent to:
OECD Publications Service, 2 rue André-Pascal,
75775 Paris Cedex 16, France.

Les commandes provenant de pays où l'OCDE n'a
pas encore désigné de distributeur peuvent être
adressées à : OCDE, Service des Publications,
2, rue André-Pascal, 75775 Paris Cedex 16, France.

1-1995

OECD PUBLICATIONS, 2 rue André-Pascal, 75775 PARIS CEDEX 16
PRINTED IN FRANCE
(91 95 04 3) ISBN 92-64-04356-X - No. 47794 1995